KU-520-774

Ethics in Context

The Art of Dealing with Serious Questions

Gernot Böhme

Translated by Edmund Jephcott

LIVERPOOL
JOHN MOORES UNIVERSITY
AVRIL ROBARTS LRC
TEL. 0151 231 4022

Polity

Copyright © this translation Polity Press 2001
First published in Germany as Gernot Böhme, *Ethik im Kontext: Über den Umgang mit ernsten Fragen*, © Suhrkamp Verlag Frankfurt am Main 1997

First published in 2001 by Polity Press in association with Blackwell Publishers Ltd.

Published with the assistance of the Max-Himmelheber Stiftung and the Professor Dr Alfred Schmid Stiftung.

Editorial office:
Polity Press
65 Bridge Street
Cambridge CB2 1UR, UK

Marketing and production:
Blackwell Publishers Ltd
108 Cowley Road
Oxford OX4 1JF, UK

Published in the USA by
Blackwell Publishers Inc.
350 Main Street
Malden, MA 02148, USA

All rights reserved. Except for the quotation of short passages for the purposes of criticism and review, no part of this publication may be reproduced, stored in a retrieval system, or transmitted, in any form or by any means, electronic, mechanical, photocopying, recording or otherwise, without the prior permission of the publisher.

Except in the United States of America, this book is sold subject to the condition that it shall not, by way of trade or otherwise, be lent, re-sold, hired out, or otherwise circulated without the publisher's prior consent in any form of binding or cover other than that in which it is published and without a similar condition including this condition being imposed on the subsequent purchaser.

A catalogue record for this book is available from the British Library.

Library of Congress Cataloging-in-Publication Data
Böhme, Gernot.
    [Ethick im Kontext. English]
    Ethics in context : the art of dealing with serious questions / Gernot Böhme ; translated by Edmund Jephcott.
        p. cm.
    Includes index.
    ISBN 0-7456-2638-6—ISBN 0-7456-2639-4 (pbk.)
    1. Applied ethics. I. Title.
BJ1125 .B6413 2001
170—dc21

                                                            2001021634

Typeset in 10.5 on 12 pt Palatino
by SetSystems Ltd, Saffron Walden, Essex
Printed in Great Britain by MPG Books Ltd, Bodmin, Cornwall

This book is printed on acid-free paper.

Ethics in Context

2006

LIVERPOOL JMU LIBRARY

3 1111 00959 8226

Contents

Acknowledgements

This book evolved from a series of lectures on ethics I gave at the Technische Universität Darmstadt in the Winter Semester 1995/96. My thanks are due to my audience and students for the extensive discussions I had with them. I would also like to thank Professor Heidrun Abromeit, Darmstadt, Professor Adalbert Podlech, Darmstadt, Professor T. Maruyama, Kyoto, and Dr Christoph Rehmann, Basel, for their criticism and helpful comments on individual chapters.

We are not concerned to know what goodness is but how to become good men, since otherwise our enquiry would be useless.

Aristotle, *Nicomachean Ethics*, II, 1103b 27–9

— 1 —

Introduction

From a Critique to a New Approach:
Serious Questions

Interest in a book on ethics can be taken for granted today. That makes it all the more important to be clear from the outset about the nature of this interest. Normally, what is expected from a book is information. But is that still the case when the book is about ethics?

In posing this question one realizes that the word *interest*, which in any other subject is used without a second thought, takes on a special meaning in the case of ethics. Whereas one's interest in other subjects can be satisfied by information, so that *interest* means the same as curiosity, the situation is quite different with ethics. Ethics does not inform us about anything; it does not enlarge knowledge; it does not respond to curiosity but to a very different kind of unease. What one expects from ethics is not information but guidance. To be interested in ethics therefore means to be 'interested' in the sense of being involved, being affected. Ethics in the form of a written text occupies a peculiar position. It presupposes in the reader a personal commitment, a disquiet, a willingness to pose questions, a desire to change.

To elucidate this special position of texts on ethics, and at the same time to clarify the sense in which the term 'ethics' is used in what follows, I think it would be useful to call to mind the threefold division of philosophy which I adopted in my introduction to philosophy.[1] In my view, there are three different ways of approaching philosophy: it can be seen as a way of life, as practical wisdom and as a science. The third of these, philosophy as a science or a body of knowledge, is the one ordinarily practised at academic institutions. Philosophy is understood as an area of knowledge of a specific kind, with its own methods and schools, with a research frontier which is constantly moving forward and with special problems generated by the advance of this frontier. The manner in which this academic philosophy is presented consists essentially in argument and refutation. It shares with science the ideal of objectivity, which implies a strict division between knowledge and the person holding that knowledge: the argument is supposed to be independent of the person who puts it forward and, conversely, the person can be entirely unaffected by the knowledge he or she possesses and pursues.

I shall not approach moral philosophy in this way. That does not mean, however, that such an approach is not possible. On the contrary, one cannot help observing that the major part of what is taught at universities under the heading of ethics, moral philosophy or practical philosophy does, indeed, fall into the category of *philosophy-as-science*. In it the structure of deontic statements is examined, the speech-act of imperatives is defined, the possibility of moral arguments is studied and the legitimacy of moral judgements analysed. None of this need have anything to do with personal involvement or commitment; indeed, it does not have to affect the philosopher, or his or her listeners and readers, at the personal level at all. Quite the contrary: the less it has to do with such things, the better – that is, the more scientific. In what follows, therefore, I shall not expound academic philosophy, or what might be called the discourse of practical philosophy; nor shall I discuss its historical development, that is, the history of ethics. Indeed, I do not know what benefit readers, who, in most cases, will not be professional philosophers, might derive from such an exercise. I am aware, or course, that the broad interest in ethics today, which stems from a profound sense of unease, is fed to a large extent by the debate being conducted among academic philosophers. Later in this book, therefore, I shall touch on the history of ethics and the current academic discourse, but only when something worthwhile can be learned from it. In this introduction, though only here, I should like to comment on academic discourse and practical philosophy from a critical standpoint, in order to make clear how my approach differs from it.

Ethics, as it will be presented here, has less to do with philosophy *qua* science than with philosophy as a mode of living or a way of life, and as a body of wisdom for living. Philosophy as a mode of living is, in a certain sense, quite the opposite of philosophy as science. It is concerned with knowledge in so far as it engages with the person, with a conduct of life which is fundamentally guided by knowledge, or, more precisely, which is determined by the state of knowledge of the person concerned. The idea of a special, philosophical way of life has its prototype in the figure of Socrates.[2] Socrates demonstrated in his own person – and tried to bring about in others – a state of consciousness which provided a basis for authentic actions, and for giving an account both of one's actions and of one's existence. To lead a philosophical life is not everyone's affair; it even implies an aspiration not to be like everyone else. Nevertheless, the philosophical way of life has acted as a model for many; it has been disseminated through various media, such as education, by which it has also been trivialized. In my introduction to philosophy I showed that the modern way of living is in many respects a trivialization of the classical ideal of a philosophical conduct of life.[3] This fact alone is enough to indicate that a philosophical mode of life must be defined differently today from the one which evolved in the great line of development from Socrates to Stoicism. This, however, confronts us once more with the need to distinguish the philosophical life from the average one. Today, too, it is the case that not everyone is interested in leading a philosophical life.

If, in what follows, ethics is placed in the context of philosophy as a mode of living, that means that ethics is an enquiry into a special mode of life with special claims. And here, too, it is the case that leading a moral life is not for everyone.

The third approach to philosophy I have called, with Kant, 'practical wisdom' (*Weltweisheit*). Kant distinguishes practical wisdom from the philosophy of the schools, that is, from what I have called scientific philosophy, by saying that it is concerned with 'what interests everyone'. Consequently, philosophy as practical wisdom is, to my mind, the philosophy which engages with the problems confronting us today. Ethics in the framework of practical wisdom is therefore clearly distinguished from ethics as a philosophical mode of living. For it is concerned, precisely, with what interests and involves everyone, that is, with public questions. Accordingly, moral problems are not regarded in this case as problems of one's mode of living, but as problems of public opinion-forming and social regulation.

This way of understanding philosophy means that an account of ethics will need to be divided into two distinct parts. The first part will deal with problems of living, the question as to what a moral life consists of and how one must form oneself as a person in order to be a human being not just somehow, but *well*. The second part will be concerned with how, against what background and with what arguments one can take part in concrete discourse in order to contribute to a public process of forming opinion on moral questions, and thereby of establishing social norms. To begin with, these two parts, these different conceptions of ethics, will be starkly confronted with each other, without any attempt to soften the harshness of their juxtaposition. On one hand, philosophical living, which is not for everyone; on the other, involvement in problems which interest everyone; on one side, existence and the formation of personality; on the other, speech and argumentation. This contrast will not be glossed over, although, later, clear connections and mediations between the two sides will emerge, and will make the opposition between them more understandable and plausible.

First of all, however, I should like to set out my critique of practical philosophy as it is carried on in academic discourse, and thereby justify my decision not to base the present book concerning ethics on that discourse. This critique will take the form of four theses, each one referring to a particular tendency of academic ethics or schools of ethics:

1   *Academic ethics fails to reach the level of concrete problems.* This criticism applies above all to the so-called ethics of discourse, but also to other varieties, which see themselves as reconstructions of Kantian ethics and the 'categorical imperative'. If one takes the justification of moral judgements to be the central problem of ethics, once either confines oneself, like Kant, to purely formal statements, or, at most, one can, like Apel, extract the implicit norms from the discursive situation.[4] It is, of course, the case that by entering into a discourse one accepts certain rules and also subscribes to a mutual recognition between the partners. But it would be quite impossible to derive any guidelines for concrete living from that situation. Apel had an inkling of this, and therefore suggested what he called bridging principles, or principles of application (*Anwendungsprinzipien*),[5] the aim of which was to ensure that such a thing as practical discourse could take place at all. Nevertheless, this whole undertaking remains an ivory-tower philosophy, an ethics which fails to recognize moral problems existing *outside in the world* as relevant to its work, but is driven along instead by the increasingly sophisticated arguments of its academic practitioners. If the ethics of discourse is to have any

relevance at all, it is to the second part of ethics that I mentioned just now, the formation of a public consciousness as a background for necessary social regulations. This is how it was finally understood by Habermas, when he sought to translate the ethics of discourse into a discourse about the policy of legislation.[6]

2 *Academic ethics fails to address the difference between moral judgements and moral actions.* The academic debate on ethics is dominated, in almost all philosophical schools, by certain empirical investigations into the development of moral judgement, as carried out by Lawrence Kohlberg on the basis of Piaget's work.[7] In these investigations the authors constructed a developmental logic of moral consciousness leading from simple guidance by reward and punishment through several clearly definable stages to actions governed by principles. But – and this is the crucial point – these actions are not really actions at all, but moral judgements. Whether people who judge a given moral dilemma in such and such a way according to such and such principles would then act in accordance with their judgement in a concrete situation is a completely open question. Not only that: it is a question which is not even asked. These investigations, therefore, are not concerned with the moral development of the child or adolescent, as they claim, but, like Piaget's, with cognitive development. Large sections of moral philosophy which are strongly influenced by these analyses are also concerned solely with moral judgements. For example, Tugendhat's *Vorlesungen über Ethik* revolves around the grounds and backgrounds of moral evaluations.[8] Although he does seek to break out of the closed intellectual circle by including motives for moral judgements as well as grounds or reasons, he cannot leap the chasm between judgement and action, nor is he even interested in doing so. One might say that, since Socrates, this chasm has been the central problem of ethics. 'Do you hold knowledge to be something which rules us?' Socrates asked the Sophist Protagoras.[9] The latter believed, like most people, that while one often knows full well what the good action is, one still does not perform it, being 'overcome by desires'. Jesus Christ, in the Gospel of St Matthew, also says famously: 'The spirit is willing but the flesh is weak.' In Kant's work it was still clear that moral existence involved a struggle with one's own structure of impulses. In academic philosophy since Freud, and perhaps precisely because of Freud, there is no longer any discussion of this issue.

3 *Academic philosophy continues to propagate illusions about the relationship between virtue and happiness.* That the wicked prosper and the good do not has been a challenge to ethics from the first.

Faced by this manifest scandal, ethical reflection has striven in every conceivable way to demonstrate that it is also *advantageous* to strive for the good. Most ethical systems were unable to do without a long-term perspective, frequently extending into the after-life, in which being good finally came to the same thing as being happy. The chasm between the two is usually bridged by ambiguous talk of the *good life* or the *successful life*. One can either interpret that concept in the manner of Socrates, who maintained that tyrants were not really happy because they had a tyrannical inner constitution,[10] or one could understand it to mean that the good person who is in a bad situation can still derive enough satisfaction from his good deeds to be content. It is incomprehensible to me how anyone, after the horrors and barbarism of the twentieth century, could still cling to such threadbare consolations. It is certainly better to emphasize, with Hans Krämer,[11] that morality can prejudice the subjective striving for happiness. Krämer gives the name of *striving ethics* (*Strebensethik*) to an area of ethics explicitly directed towards self-realization and earthly goods, in which what is held to be good is defined subjectively. He, at any rate, does not give the impression, under the flimsy heading of an *ethics of the good life*, that a moral existence leads at the same time to a hedonistically fulfilled life.[12]

4   *Academic ethics fails to locate itself in the context of history and civilization within which it seeks to be effective.* I have already mentioned that academic ethics has its starting-point in academic discourses and not in current moral questions. Indeed, for the most part it should not be referred to as ethics but as meta-ethics, in that it does not discuss moral questions but is concerned with the conditions determining the possibility of such discussion, that is, with moral argumentation and reasoning. Still worse than this absence of context is its lack of any historical and social reference. The discourse of practical philosophy takes no account of the fact that it is being conducted in the twentieth century, or, more specifically, in twentieth-century Germany. When, for example, Wolfgang Kuhlmann, in his introduction to the volume *Zerstörung des moralischen Selbstbewusstseins*, claims that ethical discourse in the German Federal Republic since 1945 has been dominated by horror at the new barbarism of the twentieth century, that is pure wishful thinking. He himself admits that explicit concern over the destruction of the constitutional state and the organized mass murder in the Third Reich has *not* found its way into ethical theories (p. 16).[13] It is equally grotesque when, in the same volume, Apel explains the failure of intellectuals in the Third Reich as an

error occurring 'at the crisis stage in the transition from the morality of conventional to that of post-conventional principles'.[14] He believes, for example, that 'a *universally valid normative* principle could have preserved Heidegger from total surrender to the *kairos*'.[15] Here the horrors and wretchedness of the twentieth century are used quite extraneously to recommend one's own philosophy. There can be no question of a shattering of previously self-evident moral truths. Tugendhat thus derives the legitimacy of the state from his reformulation of the categorical imperative.[16] It passes understanding how a philosopher can be so little a contemporary of the twentieth century that in such a connection he fails to mention *state terror*, the experience of which has shaped our historical and political consciousness. In the collection mentioned, only Hans Ebeling even attempts such a thing. In his contribution, 'Vom Schrecken des Staats zum Umbau der Philosophie' [From state terror to the reconstruction of philosophy], he states that philosophical support for the state has become impossible today, and that 'refusal of assent [to the state] is not only legitimate but morally imperative'.[17]

If we look back on this fourfold critique of academic ethics, it emerges that my own enterprise in this book must meet four principal demands: ethics must

- set out from an identification of current moral problems;
- confront the difference between moral judgement and the possibility and capacity for action.

In addition, it must

- acknowledge the divergence between virtue and happiness; and, finally,
- make explicit the basic historical conditions under which moral action and argumentation take place today.

Accordingly, we must first assure ourselves that moral problems do in fact exist. That this is necessary may seem a little strange, since I began by noting that a widespread uncertainty over guidelines for living was a precondition of the present intensive discussion of ethics, and therefore of this book. Does that not mean that we all feel ourselves beset by moral problems? Clearly, these two things are not the same: the general uncertainty over guidelines can go hand in hand with an average, morally untroubled consciousness with regard to everyday matters. The reason is that everyday life and behaviour are, in general, adequately regulated by considerations of expediency and of what is *customary*. The questions as to whether one rides on a bus without paying, tells lies to one's partner or evades taxes are not, in my opinion, moral questions. They are sufficiently regulated or decidable by customary behaviour and worldly wisdom, which can sometimes simply be called shrewdness. Admittedly, there are authors who regard such questions as moral questions as well. I should therefore state that here and in what follows I use the term *moral questions* in a specific sense, to refer to questions *which concern serious matters*. This view will be explained and justified in the course of the book. For now I will say only that when I assert that there are *moral* questions, I mean that there are questions which arise at certain times when matters become serious for each of us. How we decide those questions determines who we are and what kind of people we are.

However, in terms of the division of this book set out above, I have so far stated what a moral question is for only one part of the book – the part concerned with the moral existence of the individual and the development of the individual's mode of life. The other aspect of ethics relates to the formation of public opinion as a background for necessary social regulations. Here, too, I would maintain that moral questions exist today. What does that mean in this context? By analogy with the first definition, one might say that these questions are those which arise when matters become serious for society, which decide the kind of society we live in. Certainly, that is not a bad answer. But here, too, one must first satisfy oneself that moral questions do actually exist in the sphere of social arrangements and regulations. For it could equally be the case that everything in that sphere is done according to expediency, or according to the knowledge provided by science – or simply by convention. It is not difficult to give examples of such *morality-free* social regulations. Road traffic arrangements, for example, are a matter partly of expediency and partly of convention. Accordingly, legislators attempt to base regulations concerning matters such as emissions control on purely scientific facts – for example, facts about toxicity. Of course, such attempts frequently conceal an element of convention, and some critics would contend that even definitions of emissions threshold values are moral questions, i.e. value judgements. The term 'value' is not, perhaps, a happy choice, since it can too easily carry economic connotations. But it does point in the direction from which one might expect an answer to the question as to what a moral question is in the context of public opinion formation. It is a question of social regulation which cannot arise solely through expedience or through *mere* convention, but requires a more general guideline. This general guideline can be one which a society, our society, has always possessed, i.e. one which society has adopted historically or implicitly through the form of its communal life; or it can be one which it has to arrive at by a majority decision and which becomes the basis of communal life from then on. Such basic guidelines are, in fact, often called values, or basic values – as in the debates between political parties on fundamental values, or when one speaks of the *basic values of our democracy* – or they may be referred to as fundamental rights, such as (to mention the most important example) human rights.

All this merely indicates formally what moral questions are. It has, however, already had one interesting result: it has brought to light the analogy between the two otherwise quite heterogeneous areas of ethics. A moral question in the area of ethics concerned with the formation of an individual mode of living is a question by which it is decided how a person regards himself or herself, and who that person is; a moral question in the field of the public discourse devoted to establishing social norms is a question by which it is decided how a society regards itself and what it becomes. In each case these are questions in which matters become serious for the individual person or for the society.

To support the contention that moral questions really do exist today in both areas it will be enough to give one example for each area. For the first area, a difficulty might arise from the fact that the point at which matters become serious for a particular person is highly individual and is different for each person. That is correct. It is, however, characteristic of the shared nature of our life situation that one can specify at least the dimensions within which matters become serious at some point for everyone. *One* such dimension is defined by the possibilities of technical-scientific medicine. The possibilities of manipulation made available by technical-scientific medicine are such that it is no longer clear today what the individual must accept as simply a given feature of one's corporeal existence. The need for sleep can be regulated by sedatives and stimulants, mood by other stimulants and psycho-pharmaceuticals, fitness and physique can be enhanced, aptitudes can be modified (or will be in the near future) by gene manipulation, organs can be exchanged in case of sickness and, finally, life itself can be prolonged far beyond the patient's active ability to determine its content. The range of these possibilities for manipulation is in principle unlimited; that is, there is no pre-existing definition of what must be accepted as unalterably 'given' and therefore as nature. Two moral problems are connected with this. One is that by granting unlimited scope to scientific-technical manipulation, one forfeits the possibility of self-determination. Experts decide what is to be done, within the range of what is technically feasible. It follows from this, however, that the preservation of the person as a self-determining agency requires that, at some point, one should say 'No' to this unlimited manipulation. The second problem presents itself in a similar way, although against a different background. Traditionally, humanity's way of understanding itself has been determined by the difference between nature and self-consciousness, between 'facticity' and 'project'. The moral worth of people was decided in terms of the way in which they dealt with their given physical circumstances, their dispositions, illnesses, blows of fate, and so on. But if nature itself is now at our disposal, that is, if it is no longer clear what must actually be accepted as given, the stage on which a person can prove his or her moral worth has been, in a sense, removed. As the possibilities of technical manipulation are now a part of our world as a matter of fact, one cannot deny that the boundary between nature and consciousness, facticity and project, has become movable. Yet who one is, that is to say the integrity of the person, is decided by whether and where this boundary is located. Here, again, it cannot be said in general terms that one's moral existence is decided through a struggle with one's own nature, but it can be said that it is decided by the fact that one does recognize at least something in oneself as 'nature'. This makes it clear that, for all people at some time, their moral existence is decided within this dimension, although it is an entirely individual matter *at which point* within this dimension the decision occurs.

The second example is taken from the field of social regulations. Here I shall choose the debate on euthanasia. This example has nothing to do with individual morality, but is concerned with social regulation. This regulation is necessary, on one hand, because in our society there is a general prohibition on killing, and because, more particularly, doctors are obliged by the Hippocratic oath to exercise their profession with the objective of preserving life. On the other hand, there is a need for social regulation because, in view of the possibilities of modern medicine, and especially that of intensive care, it has become possible to preserve life to an extent which, in individual cases, can lead to a humanly degrading form of existence. Another legitimation for considering a relaxation of the prohibition on killing in this case is the right of self-determination, also universally recognized. The need for social regulation has arisen, therefore, partly as a result of technical-medical developments, and thus historically, and partly as a result of a tension between two different basic values, one calling for the preservation of life and the other for self-determination. That this is a moral question is obvious: certain basic values or guidelines upheld by society as a whole are at issue. But this example also makes it clear that such moral questions can only be decided by taking account of the historical context of the debate. In this case, of course, the practice in the Third Reich of eliminating those 'unworthy of life' plays a part. It is quite impossible to decide on this question today without seeing it against the background of a misuse of the idea of euthanasia – if the practice of the Third Reich can be described even as that. What is at issue here, therefore, is not only basic values but our society's historical understanding of itself.

Looking back at these examples, I should like to note one other formal difference between them, which throws light on what can be achieved by this book on ethics, understood as a contribution to general discourse, not a personal conversation. In considering questions which effectively decide what an individual is, we can say nothing at all about the individual, but only something *general* about the dimension within which it is decided at some time what each person is. In considering the moral questions which relate to society at large, and which for that reason must be treated in the form of argument and general discourse, it has emerged that, ultimately, these questions can only be decided if one refers radically to the social *individual*, that is to say, if one refers not to society in general but to our German society.

Themes of Ethics

The field of ethics is divided up in various ways. Such classifications have to do with degrees of universality, for example. Thus, one speaks of general and specific ethics. But distinctions are also made, according to the addressee, between individual ethics and social ethics, or, according to the type of behaviour, between the ethics of striving or the ethics of virtue, and regulatory ethics or moral philosophy. Hegel's distinction between ethical life (*Sitt-lichkeit*), i.e. the norms which are implicitly followed in everyday behaviour, and morality (*Moralität*), i.e. behaviour based on prin-ciples, has been very influential. No less so was Kant's distinction between the *critique of practical reason* and the *metaphysics of morals*, the former corresponding to meta-ethics, that is, the clarification and justification of moral propositions, while the *metaphysics of morals* contains the elaboration of duties, up to and including legal regulations. The various classifications of ethics have also often been associated with terminological definitions of the terms 'ethics', 'morality', 'morals' (*Ethik, Moral, Sittlichkeit*). The attempts to give these terms, some of which have their origin in Latin, some in Greek and some in the Germanic languages, an unambiguous and restricted meaning have not succeeded in their aim, and I shall use them here in varying ways, as best suits the particular context. Meta-ethics will not be dealt with in this book. On the contrary, its declared aim is to get as close to the real moral questions as possible. Meta-ethical considerations will therefore only be intro-duced *ad hoc*, where they are needed. With regard to the practical relevance of ethics, its function as a guideline for behaviour, I would like to propose a three-part division. The first part deals with the theme of 'being-human-well', the second with the theme of customary behaviour and the third with the theme of establish-ing social conventions. Of these three parts only the first and third fall within the field of philosophy in the strict sense. To determine what is customary is the business of social psychology and cultural studies; to reinforce and propagate customary behaviour as a guideline for living is the affair of education in the widest sense. Here, in the framework of philosophical ethics, the primary focus will be on virtue and on the discursive guidelines which are intended to lead to norms of behaviour. Customary behaviour will therefore be given somewhat more extensive treatment than the other themes in this introductory presentation of the three parts. Customary behaviour stands midway between virtue and behav-ioural norms, and also has a certain function of mediating between them.

Being-human-well

What I refer to here as 'being-human-well' bore the title in classical ethics, depending on the language, of *arete*, *virtus*, or virtue. I do not use these terms, because it is no longer possible to work directly within the tradition they represent. Although there has recently been a renascence or rehabilitation of 'virtues' in English-language philosophy,[18] it will not be possible to revive the equivalent term *Tugend* in German. It has been too seriously devalued by the eighteenth-century catalogues of virtues and vices, and the prudery of the Victorian age. The word 'virtuous' (*tugendhaft*) calls to mind a bashful young girl rather than a virile young man.

For my purposes, the same still applies to 'virtue' in English. When I speak, instead, of 'being-human-well', I seek to invoke the original meaning and scope of the Greek word *arete*. The Greeks spoke not just of the *arete* of a man or a woman, but of a horse or even a knife. This meaning actually emerges most clearly in connection with the *arete* – the 'goodness' – of the knife. For the goodness of the knife is not something added to its being, but is, precisely, the fact that it is 'good at being a knife'. This assumes that a knife can be what it is, a knife, more or less well. It emerges from this locution that in calling a knife good one is also calling it better than others. The same meaning is contained in the general use of the Greek term *arete*. This term is connected to the concept good, *agathos*, via the superlative form *aristos*, best.[19] The *arestoi* are the best people, the aristocrats, the rulers. It follows that whenever goodness is at issue, being better is also at issue, and that by asking about goodness one has already raised the question of comparison, of distinction from what is worse.

It can be seen at this point that the theme of 'goodness' must be distinguished from the question of customary behaviour. To be guided by customary behaviour and to conduct oneself as people usually do is the exact opposite of engaging with the dimension of comparison. Someone who conforms to customary behaviour is a good person in the sense that they are polite, reliable, inoffensive. To call someone a good person in the context of the customary has an almost pejorative connotation: he or she is innocuous, incapable of causing a stir but, at any rate, amenable enough.

In the everyday locution about good people the idea 'good' has not yet become part of 'being human'. It is a kind of additional predicate, a quality. But when I refer to 'goodness' as the first theme of ethics, I do not mean that a person is designated as good according to this or that criterion, but that he or she *is a person well*. Goodness refers here, therefore, to an inner possibility of comparison, or heightening, or development, towards a perfectibility within the person, towards the humanity of the person which is to be developed.

The term 'goodness' in the sense of being-human-well thus presupposes a quite specific way of looking at the human being, a specific type of self-understanding, a philosophical anthropology. Of course, everyone whom one encounters empirically is a *human being*, and it is extremely important to keep this in mind; it is also possible to content oneself with empirical existence and to confine oneself in general to customary behaviour. But discourse about being-human-well presupposes within our understanding of the human being, or introduces into it, a difference between what the human being is empirically and what he or she really ought to or could be. In his lectures on anthropology Kant characterized this difference by saying that he was speaking of anthropology both in the physical and in the pragmatic sense. Anthropology in the physical sense deals with human beings as they exist, as one actually finds them and as they find themselves, whereas anthropology in the pragmatic sense refers to human beings with regard to that which they can make of themselves. It can be seen that in speaking about a person's goodness in the sense of being a human well, and thus about a crucial portion of ethics, one is concerned with a rift or fissure running through human existence, an inner danger, a risky undertaking which will not necessarily meet with success. It may be, also, that one has to take account of evil as a specific power – I shall come back to that. But what emerges here is that in setting out towards being-human-well one encounters dangers along the way. Sophocles's statement that 'of all things man is the most terrible'[20] already suggests something of this ambivalence. The term he uses, *deinoteros*, means more capable, more powerful, as well as more terrible. A being who is not content with the way he finds himself is a being at risk.

The striving to be good always presupposes an idea of what a human being 'properly' is, an idea of the ideal human being. To achieve goodness means to heighten one's being, to raise oneself out of empirical indeterminacy. The heightening of human existence towards an ideal has always entailed an increase in one-sidedness, a certain narrowing. The so-called virtues – bravery, self-mastery, chastity, etc. – were dimensions of this narrowing. Certainly, humanism, with its idea of all-round education, did something to counteract this tendency, though it did so at the price of failing to recognize that heightening always also involves loss. Nevertheless, it did perceive correctly that the striving for heightened humanity always contains a tendency towards hubris. Nietzsche gave expression to this tendency in his concept of the *Übermensch*. In the Third Reich this concept, in combination with racist ideas, brought forth its corollary, the concept of the subhuman being, and a praxis based on contempt for humanity. We have every reason today to include in the idea of human goodness a recognition of the dependencies and fragility of human beings.

To be a human being well means consciously to appropriate, explicate and intensify what it is to be human. For this reason, this aspect of ethics always has a relationship to anthropology, although to a philosophical anthropology, i.e. to the elaboration of a human self-understanding. We shall have to concern ourselves with the question whether that means tying ethics back into metaphysics, into concepts of being, or tying it to nature, as in speaking of natural rights as rights 'which are born with us'. I believe that a pragmatic conception of anthropology enables us to avoid these implications. What is ordinarily called the *essence of man* consists only of historically conditioned self-images or ideals of the human being, which one uses to set oneself apart from one's given empirical existence. We shall not be concerned with such ideals of human existence in ethics, but with the difference which underlies their emergence – the difference between facticity and project, or, in more traditional terms, between nature and freedom. To be a human being well means to expose oneself fully to this difference, and not just to be guided one-sidedly and therefore blindly by a human ideal, whether it be reason, 'being-a-person' or freedom; but it also means to be able to accept and live out facticity, one's given existence, the fact that one is not the ground of one's own self. To be human well means also to be nature, to be aware of one's dependence on history and other human beings, to be aware that one does not represent humanity *on one's own*, but that, through the very striving for intensification, one becomes one-sided and therefore in need of completion by others. It is precisely this which distinguishes being-human-well from the traditional ideal of 'the good person', and from the traditional ideals of an ethics of striving. The body as the nature which we ourselves are, feelings which come over us and take possession of us and thereby cause us to be engaged in the world, our dependence on a livelihood and on recognition by others – all these are essential parts of the human condition, and to be able to live out these conditions is just as much a part of being-human-well as the formation of will and responsibility for our actions.

Customary behaviour

Customary behaviour refers to those things *one does*, which are required by custom, which are expected of us. Traditionally, the sphere of customary behaviour was called *ethos* or *mores*. But it would be quite mistaken to describe this sphere as that of morality in the proper sense. Morality only arises when, for good reasons, one deviates from customary behaviour, or prepares for new common practices by challenging the existing ones. The sphere of customary behaviour is therefore one in which neither moral decisions nor moral argumentation is required. It thus has no need of philosophy, though it does need the sphere of education in order to propagate itself.

If this characterization might appear to confer second-rank status on the sphere of customary behaviour, since it contains no moral challenges, that impression should be revised at once. For it is customary behaviour which regulates our ordinary conduct and relieves us of the need for decisions and justifications in our everyday lives. And it is also customary behaviour which affects the greater mass of people. While it is not everyone's affair to lead a moral life or to participate in practical discourse, everyone is nevertheless guided generally by customary behaviour. For this reason, the functional expectations placed on ethics can best be achieved through customary behaviour. And the hopes placed on ethics are, indeed, high. Environmental ethics is expected to put a stop to ecological destruction, peace ethics is expected to prevent wars, scientific and technical ethics is expected to direct these potentialities for the benefit of humanity. Too much, in fact, is expected of ethics, especially if the expectations are directed at the sense of responsibility or at actions guided by principle. The world is not changed by morality, and, moreover, it would be a degradation of morality to place on it demands for functional benefits. Changes to customary behaviour, on the other hand, can be effective. And it in no way detracts from customary behaviour to justify it by its usefulness. For example, it does actually make a difference whether or not it is customary in a culture to wrap each gift in paper. It will make a difference if it is frowned upon to get in a car each time one goes to post a letter. And it will make a difference for the entire system of water distribution whether or not it is customary within a national society to take a shower in the morning. Precisely because customary behaviour is effective on a mass scale, it can perform certain functions through its effects and side-effects. It is important to note, however, that behaviour in accordance with custom, or against it, in no way depends on the moral justification of customary behaviour. It is sufficient that the behaviour is, or is not, required by custom.

One does not conform to customary practices in one's behaviour because they are *moral*, but because infringement of them is penalized. Someone who does not respect customary practices is noticed, viewed with suspicion, 'does not fit in' and, in some cases, especially if the person concerned is a child, is admonished or punished. Customary practices must, however, be distinguished from laws. They are much like unwritten laws; they have unofficial validity and are not enforced by public authorities. A person's moral existence does not depend on them, but his or her social status and reputation certainly do. For this reason the most general heading under which customary behaviour can be placed is that of *respectability*.

This term, too, has slightly pejorative connotations. Respectability is not morality; it can be upheld merely for the sake of appearance, or for opportunistic reasons. To give substance to this formulation, a number of customary practices, or species of such practices, will be listed.

First of all, there is politeness:[21] it is customary to be polite towards other people, especially strangers. The rules of politeness preserve a certain distance and ensure that one's interlocutors are acknowledged and treated with respect. They also imply that one is attentive, obliging and considerate towards their personhood, especially their sense of *honour*.

The example of politeness allows us to study two characteristics which reappear in analogous form in other forms of customary behaviour. First, the restricted, perspectival application of politeness. Politeness first came into being as a form of conduct among equals, the nobility, the court society – hence the term 'courtesy'. That is typical of customary behaviour. What is customary is customary *here for us*, or *among us*, in this region or in this firm. Although politeness has been disseminated by the social mechanism of imitation through all strata of society,[22] it is characteristic that as late as Kant's time the German bourgeoisie expressed opposition to 'courtesy' (*Höflichkeit*) and attempted to replace it with 'urbanity' (*Urbanität*). Even though courtesy is no longer class-specific today, it is perspectival: one relates politely to others in particular respects. Polite behaviour is not a direct or intimate form of behaviour. This means that in personal relationships in which politeness is suspended through lack of distance, behaviour may be much more authentic than in relation to strangers, but it may also be much more brutal. In saying this we have touched on the other characteristic of customary behaviour – what can be referred to critically as its inauthenticity. If I am guided by customary behaviour, I do *what people do*. That can mean that I am not authentic in my behaviour, and therefore not moral; moreover, it may be that what people do is to be regarded as immoral from the standpoint of general principles.

That would not be assumed in the case of ordinary politeness. But it becomes more problematic in the case of loyalty. It is customary to be *loyal*, i.e. loyal towards the state in which one lives, the institution one serves, and towards the partners with whom one collaborates. Loyalty is one of the forms of customary behaviour which best enable us to see that such behaviour is basic to the functioning of society. To be loyal means that one does what is expected by the community *of one's own accord*, i.e. without compulsion. Loyalty is therefore, in principle, particularistic. It does not depend on a test to establish whether the community's expectations are legitimate.

Commitment should be seen as closely related to loyalty. One is expected to be committed to the institution by which one is employed, to champion its cause, to pursue its objectives. There are cases in which one is required to confirm this commitment by a promise or an oath. But as a rule it is simply customary, and if one does not conform to this customary behaviour one is dismissed. The efficiency of a firm depends on the commitment of its employees.

I come now to a number of forms of customary behaviour which have a far more moral appearance: responsibility, fidelity and solidarity. These could, it is true, be referred to as virtues in the traditional sense, or they could be lived out in our sense as forms of being-human-well. Normally, however, they are no more than customary behaviour. Responsibility in politics does not refer to far-sighted or even caring behaviour, but simply means that one must answer for what happens in one's department. And answering for it does not imply that one is bound to make good any damage, but merely that one leaves one's post: to take political responsibility means vacating one's seat for someone else and drawing one's pension in peace.

Active fidelity can be a great deal more than mere customary behaviour. But as it is normally lived, fidelity has little to do with one's actual feelings: one simply does not have 'affairs'. The status of fidelity as customary behaviour can be seen particularly clearly from the fact that its infringement, an affair, does not put an end to it; on the contrary, no effort is spared to preserve fidelity as the semblance which it is.

Lastly, solidarity. Solidarity can, it is true, be a dimension of being-human-well. But the average form of solidarity, and thus the form which has an essentially broad and collective effect, is no more than customary behaviour. Everyone is willing to be affected by what affects the others – I mean the relevant others, such as family members. No special moral effort is normally required for this. Especially in its customary form, solidarity enables us to see that customary behaviour is by no means contemptible, and can even move individuals to make significant sacrifices – if such a term may be used in this case. But solidarity as customary behaviour has limited influence, and usually does not go beyond allegiance to small groups, a family, a neighbourhood, an association.[23] Customary solidarity should therefore be distinguished radically from the demands of charity. For the latter requires us to be affected by what befalls *anyone*.

As a last example of customary behaviour I should like to mention honesty. It is customary to tell the truth because communication as information or, more correctly, as a system for exchanging statements, would otherwise not function. It is astonishing that Kant sought to use this functional argument to justify the prohibition on lying as a *moral* prohibition. But, as we have already said, expediency disregards morality. To tell the truth is *merely* customary. This can be seen from the difference between cultures on this point, a difference which, at the least, is one of degree. Even in our culture politeness is a form of customary behaviour which can have a strained relationship with honesty. Honesty is expected so that statements can normally be relied on. For this reason, honesty is enforced by admonition and sanctions.

I shall not say anything further about the area of customary behaviour. It is not of central interest to a philosophy of ethics. Indirectly, however, it will always be relevant. In a sense, what is customary is the preliminary stage of morality proper. Anyone who does not know what *people* do, and who has not mastered the area of customary behaviour, will hardly be able to go legitimately beyond it. And in the absence of deeper insight, or a commitment to something more far-reaching, it is always best to abide by what is customary. Politeness is paradigmatic of this. A polite relationship to another person is certainly not in itself an *authentic* relationship, and falls far short of personal engagement and encounter.

But, given the high level of risk which is entailed in any personal encounter, it is always advisable to remain at least polite, or to keep open the way for a return to the level of polite intercourse. Moreover, as I have already emphasized, the mass-efficacy of ethics is only possible through customary behaviour. On the other hand, there is always a danger that customary behaviour will become a vehicle for inhumanity. This danger results from the generally restricted nature of the group upholding customary behaviour – a social stratum or class, an ethnic group – and from its historically and politically conditioned character. I need only recall that at certain times it was not customary in Germany 'to patronize Jewish shops' or to marry one's daughter to 'a member of a different religion'. In my youth it was still customary to beat children at school; in South America and Africa it is customary to circumcise women. And in Germany it is customary to regard contraception as the woman's concern.[24] It can be seen from these examples that morality only really begins where one breaches customary behaviour, or works to change it.

Moral judgement and moral argument

It is generally believed that ethics has to do with action. Yet the subject matter of ethical theory and of practical ethical discourse is judgement of good and bad, right and wrong. The fact that ethics as theory and discourse is concerned with moral judgement, with moral argumentation, could easily lead to the view that it is actually irrelevant to action. For nothing guarantees that someone will act as they think, or that their capacity for judgement is in harmony with their ability to act. This confusion can be removed by making some basic distinctions. Moral discourse has, indeed, nothing to do with the individual's capacity for moral actions. The ability to act depends on very different capabilities than does the ability to judge. And moral judgement and moral argumentation take place in a very different sphere, and have a quite different goal, to that of moral action.

Moral judgement and moral argument form part of the field of public opinion-formation. Sanctions, and therefore pressure to respect customary behaviour, can be applied through public opinion. But customary behaviour can also be altered by public opinion. That is even the most important function of moral argumentation. It serves to problematize customary behaviour, or in some cases to legitimize it, or to prepare new forms of customary behaviour and build a consensus for them. This consensus can give rise to legal regulations. Conversely, the process of legislation which is carried on through parliament and public opinion frequently requires moral justifications. Legislation is by no means just a matter of convention. If it merely called for agreement, it could be arbitrary or simply an affair of the majority. In fact, however, what can be agreed upon is embedded in a context of moral conceptions, and, prior to agreement, arguments for this or that possibility are conducted on the basis of those conceptions. What the moral conceptions are, and which background contexts are being referred to in moral argumentation, generally becomes clear in the course of the discussion. They may be very deep-seated taboos, or basic values of the society in which one lives, or they may be human rights, or traditional, customary practices. In all cases, therefore, it must be said that moral arguments link conventions to a background of moral conceptions. These conceptions are never 'ultimate justifications' derived from some supreme or final principle, but are only the justifications which are necessary and called for during the argument. In the context of an argument in which certain questions are in contention, the argument will be carried on until a background on which the participants are agreed has been found, and on the basis of which the conventions under discussion can be debated. As a rule this background is rich and diffuse, not poor and specific. In this respect Apel's strategy of final justifications does not seem to meet the needs of real practical discourses. Moral competence as a capacity for judgement and argumentation consists, above all, in being able to relate existing problems to such backgrounds in regulating social praxis.

Of course, there are moral arguments which relate to particular actions. They arise when an actor or wrongdoer is called upon to justify an action, for example in court. Admittedly, the nature of trials is normally such that they are primarily concerned with ascertaining facts, which are then assessed in relation to laws, while moral arguments are used rather as qualifications to heighten or moderate the incrimination of the culprit. They are therefore usually put forward not by the defendant but by their counsel or the counsel for the prosecution. Corresponding more closely to the situation of moral justification is the everyday making of *excuses*. Here, one is concerned, for example, to justify one's failure to meet the expectations of others. In doing so, one will have to appeal to shared basic moral ideas. Structurally, therefore, the case is not different to that of the argumentation for certain regulatory standards, but it has an interest of its own in that the moral justification one gives for an action can be fundamentally different to the reasons for which the action has been carried out. Incidentally, the central objective of Kant's categorical imperative is to equate these two things – the moral arguments for an action and the reasons for carrying it out. This takes us back to the first part, to the question whether moral existence can actually be determined in that way.

The moral evaluation of particular actions and their moral justification do, in fact, play a major part in everyday life. The background of ideas to which reference is made in such justifications is not, however, very far removed from the actions. As a rule, the ideas relate to customary behaviour. At the moment when one goes beyond this background, the argument about particular actions turns into one about the legitimacy of customary behaviour itself. That is to say, the argument reverts to the one referred to as the first case – that moral arguments are those which lead to new social conventions relating to behavioural norms.

If I said earlier that moral arguments link behavioural norms to a background of basic moral ideas, that might be misunderstood to mean that I was simply talking about a transition to a higher level of generality, a transition, one might say, from laws to principles. That is indeed the case, but I also meant more than that. For the background one refers to is not only a background of principles but of concrete historical conditions. Both in the formation of social conventions and in the justification of particular actions, both of these, principles and situational background conditions, play a part. There can be a certain tension between them. At any rate, modes of argumentation can differ, depending on whether they give greater weight to principles or to situational conditions. In the debate about Kohlberg's stages in the formation of moral judgement these two alternatives were divided – not very felicitously – between male and female moral judgement.[25] That might give rise to hopes that, in considering social conventions as well as in judging individual actions, the best results would be achieved through a co-operation between men and women. Independently of any such considerations of differing competences in moral judgement, it can be said, at any rate, that a purely universalist morality cannot represent the truth. Rather, it is always necessary to take account of the historical and social context in which moral questions are posed and moral conventions are negotiated.

— 2 —

The Context of Moral Living and Argumentation

The State of Civilization

Statements about the project of being-human-well, and about the possibility and necessity of moral argumentation, must begin by taking account of the state of being human which forms the context of those statements. The historical background against which they are made must also be considered. Since the eighteenth century the section of humanity to which we belong has referred to its present state as 'civilization'. Underlying this self-evaluation was an assumption about the broad trend of human development which we can no longer accept. Europeans regarded themselves as civilized in contrast to savages and primitive peoples who lived close to nature. They believed they could define themselves in terms of their distance from nature. This meant, in the first place, their distance from their own nature, but it also implied emancipation from external nature, through controlling it.

The state of being 'civilized' was therefore distinguished from nature as a whole, and referred to a condition of human beings in which their humanity was thought to be enhanced, or even only achieved in the first place, through self-control and distancing. On the other hand, being civilized was also understood as just *one* step towards a humanity which was yet to be produced. Kant divided the development of humanity – a development through which human beings were to become truly human for the first time – into three stages: civilization, culture and morality. We no longer share the optimism of the Enlightenment, which enabled Kant to pose the question 'whether the human race is engaged in a constant progression towards a better state'.[1] The shock of the last century, caused by the outbreak of a new barbarism in Europe, the horror that such a thing was possible among 'civilized peoples', has been too profound. Nevertheless, the state of humanity which we must take as our starting-point from an ethical standpoint must be referred to as a civilized state. But this state can no longer be described in terms of progress; it must be defined quite simply as a structure both of the internal organization of human beings and of their external circumstances. If this is done, it might also become clear that the danger of the new barbarism was inherent in this very organization of human existence.

Civilization has always been characterized by its analysts as a process, not a state – as when Max Weber speaks of a process of rationalization and Norbert Elias of the 'civilizing process'. This description is not inadmissible, provided it is understood, not as an account of human history in general, but as the line of development followed by European people. It also has the advantage that a number of recent developments can be described, under the heading of *technical civilization*, as a continuation, a modification or a reversal of the civilizing process.

This book is concerned with an ethics of technical civilization. That implies that the meaning of the concept of *being-human-well* must be elaborated against the background of the state of technical civilization, and that the necessary regulating mechanisms which must be justified morally by ethical discourse arise from this state. An ethics in which a moral question is defined as one by which it is decided, for the individual, what kind of a human being he or she is, and for society, what kind of a society it is, posits the human being in a radical sense as an historical being. It is embedded in an historical anthropology. It is not an ethics in the universal sense, but an ethics of technical civilization.

When we speak today, in an ethical context, of entities such as body and soul, conscience, drives or, with Freud, of Ego, Id and Super-Ego, these are not historically invariable structures, but arise from a specific, historically conditioned attitude of the human being towards him- or herself. These organizational forms and structures of the human being could, in principle, differ between individuals and even be situation-dependent. But as they are mediated by processes of socialization and are constantly reinforced by interpersonal expectations and sanctions, they can be posited as the average constitution of the modern human being, and therefore of ourselves. Under the heading of *the civilizing process* Norbert Elias has described the historical genesis of such structures.

The most important dimension of the civilizing process for us is the transfer of the mechanism of behaviour-regulation from without to within. Norbert Elias shows that the repression of spontaneous behaviour, of passions and desires which originally – that is, prior to the modern age – was applied by external obstacles, authorities and force, is effected in modern people by an internal agency. The habituation to self-control was originally an attribute of people of higher social strata, especially the courtier. Today it is the factor which makes the modern human being calculable and unobtrusive. The repression of drives is so deep-seated that they are no longer able to develop into passions and become conscious. This affect-control, which is almost automatic and thus is not a moral attainment, operates in two directions. On the one hand it prevents strong desires and wishes from arising, and on the other it impedes receptivity to strong stimuli, and susceptibility to powerful feelings and impressions. This blocking of affects and stimuli has been inculcated since the eighteenth century, when it was directed primarily – in a way which is hardly comprehensible today – against imagination. Even at the beginning of that century imagination had been regarded as a receptivity to images, a capacity for picturing something, and thus as the faculty of sympathy, or of compassion and empathy for others. The product of this twofold, habitual affect-control is what we encounter as bourgeois emotional coolness, but also the objectivity which is characteristic of modern people. To refer to such people as bourgeois or citizens is, however, anachronistic, as we are concerned, rather, with the modern transport user and professional person. This type of person – that is, ourselves – is distinguished by a very high degree of functional usefulness; mobility and flexibility, in addition to the traditional values of punctuality, discretion, reliability and willingness to perform, are further intensifications of this type. To the independence from drives and stimuli they add a severance from regional and family ties.

Now, one might think that this highly disciplined human being – which we are – would be entirely satisfactory from the ethical point of view, and indeed, such an individual seems hardly in need of ethics at all. For ethics earlier served primarily to discipline the appetites, and to be moral meant to renounce their satisfaction in favour of higher principles. Reading old novels, dramas or educational books, one is surprised to see what moral exertion it cost to overcome the vices of unpunctuality and laziness. That is truly remarkable, in view of the ease with which the everyday demands of travel and work are met today. Nevertheless, this result of the human process of self-production – which has produced us – is not satisfactory. That has been shown by the outbreak of barbarism in the last century, both in the form of a chaotic eruption of instinctual energies and in the unresisting availability of this modern professional, transport-using human type for state-organized crime. We shall have to come back to this later.

The second dimension of the civilizing process which is relevant to our discussion is called by Norbert Elias the advance of the shame-frontier. In the centuries since the early modern period Elias has noted a progressive distancing from nature, a lengthening of the chains of mediation between nature and bodily experience, a suppression and concealment of one's own naturalness, which is relegated to an invisible, private sphere. This civilizing strategy of distancing from nature and one's natural being includes the differentiation between private and public in general, and, in particular, the internal subdividing of living spaces, the establishment of public lavatories, the use of the handkerchief, cutlery and serviettes, and table manners generally. These civilizing 'attainments' are now taken for granted, and in the age of *technical* civilization have been heightened still further – for example, by the shower, the electric razor and the deodorant. However – as Norbert Elias was clearly not yet able to perceive – the transition to *technical* civilization has caused a weakening, if not a reversal, of the main trend of the civilizing process. The objections to Elias are obvious: the emergence of nudism, the relaxation of morals in the sexual sphere, the liberalization of table manners. Even the level of domestic hygiene has long since passed its peak. Alerted by such phenomena, one discovers a downturn or a reversal in other dimensions of the civilizing process. Compared to its level in the Victorian age or the time of Freud, internal repression, too, is much reduced, since it has been taken over again by external agencies. Admittedly, repression now emanates less than earlier from direct authority or the police truncheon; rather, it is imposed by the technicization of life itself, by the general rhythm of traffic and the objective compulsions of the world of work. This does not lead, however, to a liberation of the drive-structure or the development of new passions, but to a split: whereas the life of work and travel runs its course in the cool, disciplined way called for by the modern age, and social reality is frictionless and safe, the liberalized inner world unfolds in a fictitious space: the drive-structure, freed from sanctions, no longer seeks its fulfilment in reality but in the imaginary world of the media. This equilibrium of disciplined reality-behaviour and aesthetic gratification could be regarded, from the ethical standpoint, as a satisfactory way of managing the human condition – if it were not highly unstable. In reality, the smooth organization of the public person can be seen frequently to be accompanied by a barbarization of the private sphere, and also by a devastating interaction between imaginary drive-satisfaction and the outbreak of real drive-energies in private. A characteristic example is the link between the production of pornographic films and child abuse.

A third dimension of our state of civilization can no longer be described in Elias's terms, but is determined explicitly by technology, through the existence of material systems of means. If 'technology' is understood to mean knowledge which serves production, or a regulatory system intended to enhance behavioural efficiency, then technology is a part of modernity or of the civilizing process as a whole. But for centuries technology in this sense was dependent on the disciplining and systematic training of human faculties – both physical and mental – and on the organization of communal life. In our century, technology has existed increasingly as a material system of means to which production and efficiency-enhancement could be *delegated* for any desired purpose. Technology in this sense takes on the character of an infrastructure for human and social behaviour. Thus, the nature and performance of this behaviour are co-determined by the technology existing at a given time. This process of the technical modification of human behaviour and social relationships can be referred to as technicization. It defines the current state of the civilizing process.

The relevance to ethics of this structure, which I have formulated to begin with in abstract terms, will be made clear at once by an example from sexual morality. For centuries in Europe birth control, to the extent that it was not taken care of by natural factors in any case, i.e. infant mortality, epidemics and wars, was, from the sociological standpoint, a matter of morality. The value placed on virginity, i.e. the prohibition on premarital sexual intercourse, the Christian recommendation of abstinence, the institution of celibacy and the restriction of the right to marry to those of a certain social status, had the effect of keeping the birth-rate relatively low. The population theorist Malthus, who in the early nineteenth century was the first to recognize the danger of exponential population growth and a divergence between the graphs of food production and population increase, still recommended a *moral* solution to the problem: abstinence. Today the situation is determined by the existence of *material systems of means*, that is, by technical means of contraception. As the goal of birth-limitation can be achieved directly by technical means, it no longer needs to result indirectly as a by-product of moral behaviour. This has made sexual morality largely superfluous. And its institutions, from virginity through marriage to celibacy, are becoming dispensable. This certainly does not turn sexuality into a morality-free zone. But, as compared to the nineteenth century, for example, an extensive liberalization can clearly be observed, going hand in hand with the technicizing of this sphere. And the moral questions no longer relate to distance and inner disciplining, but to which contraceptives should be used when and by which sexual partner.

So much for the description of the make-up of the modern human being as a product of technical civilization. It is probably clear from this that the question as to what it means *to be human well* cannot be answered universally and in an historically invariant form, but must be related to this make-up of ours. We have to start from ourselves as modern professional men and women and highly controlled traffic participants, with an ego-structure developed to the point of self-forgetfulness, with a highly effective mechanism for the repression or splitting-off of drive energies – people capable in principle of a high degree of objectivity, cool to the point of being inaccessible to emotion and accustomed to achieving our performances and goals not by moral exertion but by the application of technical means.

To say this, however, is to mention only the general conditions of present-day ethics, as far as they can be defined by anthropology or, better, historical anthropology. The social conditions, which have no less impact on what ethics can be today, must also be identified. I shall give an example straight away. The intense public attention now paid to ethics, the *demand* which writers on ethics can count on for their products, results from the expectation that many of the social problems which afflict us today – environmental destruction, contamination of foodstuffs, poverty, war, migration, population growth – can be solved by *ethical* behaviour. That such an expectation might be an anachronism is suggested, perhaps, by the reference to Malthus. If the aim is to protect consumers from genetically manipulated foods treated with dubious preservatives, a commercial ethics based on the idea of the *honest merchant* will have little success. The system-goal of a foodstuffs dealer is neither the nourishment nor the health of his customers, but the maximization of his profit. Why is that so, and why do these two objectives fail to coincide?

The answer is given by the general conditions of our society, the emergence of which Max Weber characterized by the concept of *rationalization*. This development correlates in many respects with the one described by Elias under the heading of *civilization*, except that it relates more to the organization of the general life of a society and its institutions, and less, as in Elias, to the inner organization of the human being. A link between the two is formed by the emergence of the modern state, which also plays a major part in Elias. The development of the modern state is determined on the one hand by the monopolization of power and on the other by the depersonalization or objectification of rule. The monopolization of power by the organs of state leads to an internal pacification of social life and to the establishment of non-violent forms of conflict-regulation between states. The neutralization or objectification of rule is attained by the establishment of the modern professional bureaucracy and the tendency of the state to be transformed into an administrative machine. This leads to a demoralization both of the relationship of the citizen to the state and of state actions. The relationships between citizen and state are no longer determined by moral categories such as welfare or loyalty, but by formally regulated rights and duties.

Max Weber characterizes the main line of development of modernity by the concept of *rationalization*. This term means that each area of life is permeated by analysis, organized according to efficiency-enhancing rules and finally monitored for success. Max Weber's model here is the rational business based on double-entry book-keeping. This kind of business is no longer concerned, like any form of economic activity, with profit, but with profitability, i.e. the intensified exploitation of capital. In the modern age, however, rationalization has changed not only businesses but practically every area of human activity – science, art, the armed forces, administration. According to Weber's cultural and socio-historical investigations, rationalization has its origin in forms of living, and influences them retroactively. In his book *The Protestant Ethic and the Spirit of Capitalism*[2] he shows that what he calls intramundane asceticism has, on one hand, generated the capacity to work – work becomes a value in itself and is not directly linked to needs and their satisfaction – and, on the other, has led to a separation of consumption from the maximization of profit. Only the latter has made possible the accumulation of capital necessary to the existence of capitalism: profits are not, as a rule, used to increase consumption, but are invested.

Max Weber thus identifies the foundations of the processes of rationalization which lead to the social conditions we call modern. They are related to those characterized by Elias: self-control, the formation of objectivity and far-sightedness, i.e. a capacity to plan and work enabling the appropriate performance of objective tasks within prescribed times, and the separation of the private and public spheres, household and business, work and leisure. However, the rationalization of all areas of society has a retroactive influence on modes of living. The first mechanism through which this takes place is the spread of expertise. Because every sphere of life, and the actions relevant to it, requires a degree of specialized knowledge so that the actions can be carried out rationally and appropriately, experts responsible for each sphere come into being, and the actions are delegated to them. This is true of spiritual and psychological care, of education, of the treatment of bodily conditions and disorders; it is true of welfare, of care in old age, of one's relationship to the state and of public relationships to other people. The development of various forms of dietetics, i.e. methods of rational living, makes the individual dependent on a host of life-advisers. As a result of the rationalization processes which constitute modernity, therefore, the situation of the individual is characterized by an almost complete incapacitation. As most actions in life require professional knowledge, the individual has to delegate them to experts. Lacking this knowledge, he or she cannot really judge and share in the experts' decisions, and, through fear of unknown risks, is only too willing to hand over his or her decisions in personal conflicts, in educational tasks, in matters of therapy, in the prosecution of rights and the meeting of demands, to specialists. It is revealing that Kant, at the end of the Enlightenment – at the end, be it noted – attributed the failure of human beings to attain intellectual majority to their dependence on experts. In his treatise 'An Answer to the Question: What Is Enlightenment?' of 1783 he writes: 'It is so easy to be immature. If I have a book that has understanding for me, a pastor who has a conscience for me, a doctor who judges my diet for me, and so forth, surely I do not need to trouble myself. I have no need to think, if only I can pay; others will take over the tedious business for me.'[3] This situation has not changed since, and has even been consolidated.

The second mechanism through which the rationalization of social life retroactively influences modes of living is the increasing differentiation of the individual spheres of life. A number of examples of this have already been mentioned – such as the separation of household and business, that is, of the reproduction sector from the production sector, and the corresponding severance of the increase in consumption from the increase in profitability. More generally, it can be said that rationalization enforces a separation of the different spheres of life and of social activity, since only in this way can they be rationally organized to meet their specific objectives. Thus, scientific activity is separated from the rest of society in that it is concerned solely with the production of truths and the reciprocal acknowledgement of their producers. Business and industry make themselves autonomous *vis-à-vis* the rest of society in that they are no longer defined from outside as a system for the satisfaction of needs, but by their internal system-objective of increased profitability. Habermas, influenced by sociological system-theorists, has described this process as the differentiation of *subsystems of instrumental action*.[4] This means that partial systems organized in terms of a particular system-goal, and in which people's behaviour is organized rationally to attain that goal, detach themselves from the – diffuse – totality of society. The resulting situation is highly significant in guiding the actions of the modern human being. What it amounts to, to state it briefly, is that the behaviour of the individual who is active within such subsystems of instrumental action is *morality-free*.

This must be clarified by an illustration. I shall take the example of the transition of agriculture to its industrialized form. Let us picture one of the old manorial estates before the industrialization of agriculture. The *lord of the manor* stood in a patriarchal relationship to the families of his labourers, who belonged to the estate even if they did not belong to him. Their payment did not take a wholly monetary form and did not depend strictly on the time spent labouring, but consisted partly in produce sufficient for subsistence, and in the provision of parcels of land for their own production. It was not the labourer or his wife as individuals who were *in service*, but the whole family, who joined in the work when needed. Conversely, the *patriarch* also felt responsible for his labourers' families, supported them in times of need, made arrangements for marriages and funerals. The relationship of the lord of the manor to nature, to his land, was a relationship to an *ancestral seat*. The working and exploitation of the land, of the fields and forests, served at the same time to reproduce them, and therefore followed well-tried rules of crop rotation, allowing fields to lie fallow, reforestation, etc. After the industrialization of agriculture the landowner's relationship to his land and workers became completely different. Let us suppose that, through impoverishment, the lord of the manor has to sell his estate to an industrialist, or that he or his family introduce industrialization themselves. In either case, *after* this moment the land becomes a capital which must yield a profit. It is cultivated according to market laws and profitability is pushed as high as possible by the use of machines and chemical fertilizers. If the estate proves no longer profitable the capital will be withdrawn and will seek other possibilities of *its* reproduction. In this process the labourers become for the first time free wage-labourers who are paid by the hour and are employed in greater or smaller numbers depending on the productivity of labour.

From an ethical standpoint the difference between these two economic forms is as follows: the lord of the manor and his actions are encompassed within a diffuse situation governed by ethics. His activity itself is not external to him; rather, what he is as a human being is decided by his conduct as lord of the manor. Accordingly, his people are not treated in a merely functional way as providers of labour power, but are also recognized in their dependent position as humans, albeit on a lower level. Even the landlord's relationship to the land and soil is a quasi-ethical one, in that it is a tradition imposing duties on him and also includes a responsibility towards the reproduction of nature. The capitalist, by contrast, is, as such, a participant in a highly differentiated system of instrumental action. His economic management is not concerned at all with moral questions, but with questions of efficiency and profitability. These factors govern his actions. And in his actions he does not stand or fall as a person, any more than his workers are integrated as persons in this instrumental context. They, like him, are mere functions, and they can – provided they have enough strength left – be *completely different people* outside the system.

This example illustrates the extraordinary significance which the process of the differentiation of social subsystems organized on instrumental principles has for ethics. It teaches us that it is pointless to try to solve the problems created by these systems with moral exhortations. The most important historical example of this is the insensitivity of the world-wide system of arms research to appeals to the *responsibility of the scientist*. One might have hoped that, in this case, the basic guidelines of the scientific system would have generated some receptivity to such appeals. The sociologist of science Robert K. Merton has named some of these basic guidelines: universalism, communalism, disinterestedness and organized scepticism.[5] Such values have indeed largely regulated the dealings of scientists with each other since the beginnings of modern science. But in practice the objectives which the scientists share with their *occupational systems*, i.e. the national research laboratory, the large research establishment, the firm, have proved dominant in relation to the universalistic standards of science. Studies by Stephen Box and Stephen Cotgrove[6] have shown that the behaviour of modern scientists is simply the behaviour of modern professional people, that is, it is finally directed not morally but instrumentally towards the system goal defined by their organizations. This situation is not refuted but is even underlined by the existence of movements such as Pugwash or the scientists' 'Responsibility for Peace' movement.

The situation of the modern human being is determined by the rationalization and differentiation of society. People participate in society primarily as professional persons. This participation consists in making their professional competence, or for a certain time their labour power, or their mere presence, available for payment. This participation has nothing to do with what they may otherwise be as human beings, or what they do in their remaining time, their so-called leisure. Their professional activity is morally irrelevant for them, in that while their income and their social status depend on it, their worth as persons, and what they amount to as human beings, do not. Conversely, their professional work serves merely as a basis for the subsistence of what they are in the rest of their lives. It affects them in no way as persons. For their family and friends their work can be entirely unknown, and as a rule it remains shadowy. They do not appear in their families in terms of their professional role – as the traditional farmer was 'the farmer' in his family as well. As a result, there is no need for present-day people to be *integral* personalities. It is sufficient if they can *switch* between their various social roles, as working people, road-users, taxpayers, family and leisure persons. In this situation the development of a personal style of life, or, indeed, self-realization, has the character of a merely private affair. It is a matter for leisure time and the private sphere. In sum: this situation is removed from the sphere of morality. The behaviour of the modern person is determined by the relevant system imperatives and by what is *customary* in the subsystem concerned, and through its lack of public relevance the project of a personal style of life is reduced to a hobby.

An ethics which is written and read in one of the developed

industrial nations of our century must take account of this situation. It is not addressed to the human being in general, but to the human being within technical civilization. This person brings with him or her a specific form of organization, has a high degree of self-control and work-capability, and separates body and soul, or, better, body and consciousness. He is not the master of his conduct of life, but is dependent on experts; he is integrated in social life as a professional and transport-using person. Social life, for its part, takes the form of a bundle of subsystems of instrumental action, which do not call on the individual as a whole person but integrate him or her only partially, i.e. functionally, and which, as a consequence, make the formation of a personal identity impossible or superfluous.

Technical civilization today largely determines what moral questions actually are; at the same time it sets the boundaries within which the individual is accessible to moral discourse, just as it also sets the boundaries within which society can be modified by moral argumentation. But it is precisely these boundaries which give moral discourse its cutting edge.

Our Historical Background

To reflect on where and when this ethics is written and read is to characterize it as an *ethics after Auschwitz*. An attempt to reconstruct, or rather to construct, Adorno's moral philosophy appeared under this title.[7] For the crucial fact is that Adorno did *not* write an ethics, and probably did not believe such a thing possible. Adorno's dictum that it is impossible to write poetry *after* Auschwitz is well known.[8] But, in fact, poetry has been written after Auschwitz, and not only after it, but in and about Auschwitz. The real meaning of Adorno's formulation is probably that poetry or an ethics after Auschwitz seemed impossible *to him*, because he felt too much solidarity with 'metaphysics at the moment of its downfall',[9] and therefore with traditional bourgeois morality. The question can only be what an ethics could look like after and under the auspices of Auschwitz. In keeping with the two main lines of ethics which were distinguished earlier, the question must be: How must I develop in order to survive morally in a world in which Auschwitz is possible? And: How must I argue morally in a country in which Auschwitz *really* existed? How must I be, what

alertness must I practise, what powers and abilities and possibilities of reflection – perhaps, indeed, what principles – must I
have at my disposal in order to survive morally in a situation in
which a whole category of people, a population group, a race, is
progressively deprived of its rights? In a situation in which I am
suddenly forbidden to go to my trusted doctor, to buy at my
traditional shop? What must I be able to do, in order to survive
morally in a situation in which my neighbours are *taken away*
nightly, colleagues are dismissed from their posts, writers and
artists are forbidden to practise their professions? What possibilities must I have at my disposal if people are insulted and
beaten up in my presence, if shops whose owners belong to a
certain category of people are looted? What will I do if I myself
am given the task or the order to remove, to deport, to shoot
people of a particular category? These are questions which are
difficult to answer in a *civilized world* and from the experience of a
civilized life. But they must be answered, and I would maintain
that our civilized life is worthless if it is not permeated by a
rehearsal of the necessary answers to such questions. That could
mean that this civilized life, which by its nature is set up to relieve
us of the burden of moral questions and claims of legitimacy,
should, case by case, be *taken seriously*.

Furthermore, how should a state and a society be structured in
a country, in a people, in which Auschwitz was a reality? How
must public institutions be judged, and how must one argue for
social regulations in a country in which, in the recent past, rights
were a racial privilege, in which, with the toleration of the whole
population and with the collaboration of a gigantic apparatus of
civil servants, employees and other participants, whole categories
of people were expelled, condemned to forced labour and mur-
dered? How must the legal system be constituted in a country in
which the right to suppress and liquidate political opponents was
exercised? How must the treatment of life, sickness and disability
be managed, when we can recall that human life was classified as
worthy and unworthy in this country, that it was degraded by
medicine into experimental material and that euthanasia was
practised to remove the burden of caring for gravely ill and
disabled people? It is these historical facts which make moral
discourse into a real discourse. They determine what can and
cannot be said, and whether this society will gain historical self-
awareness.

Social life after 1945 was not set up explicitly in terms of the
question as to how one must live in a country in which Auschwitz

had been a reality. It was set up with the desire to turn away from all that and to make a new start, although re-education and the introduction of parliamentary democracy were imposed by the western allies. The existing laws were taken over, but without the fascist additions, and especially the race laws. Their reform in line with the norms of the Basic Law proceeded slowly. Even today some laws from the pre-fascist era survive, such as the right of citizenship, which ties citizenship to descent, and therefore to *blood*. The Basic Law was created by old-style liberals and scholars, and its fundamental concepts are derived less from the experience of German history than from that of western democracies. Only from a few statutes, such as the abolition of the death penalty or the introduction of the right of resistance, and finally the original version of the right of asylum, can one gather when and for which people this Basic Law was elaborated. All the same, the fathers of the Basic Law[10] succeeded in drawing up a constitution which up to now has made possible a high degree of stability and peaceful resolution of conflicts. But the experience of German history has not been incorporated in the Basic Law sufficiently for it to be made the sole standard for further social development. Explicit remembrance of our past is necessary when we are concerned with the further development of social life and its explicit and implicit norms. This is even more the case when provisions of the Basic Law are themselves called into question, as has been the case with the right of asylum.

In the political sphere, therefore, the task of creating an ethics after Auschwitz has yet to be performed. It is no different in the individual sphere, that is, with regard to the projecting of modes of living. People from the generation of those directly involved and affected have not, as a rule, been able to synthesize their lives into a biography. We can only be lenient towards their repression, their forgetting and their silence today if we acknowledge that to assimilate and master something as terrible as what happened around them, through them and to them, was impossible. The most active of them have at least worked, through their commitment to the constitutional state and democracy, to remove the traces of the past. Nevertheless, as a result of their silence, the National-Socialist past was repressed in the public sphere in post-war Germany, and the attitude to life of the succeeding generation was *not* shaped by the legacy of Auschwitz. This was not changed when the public began to concern itself with the National-Socialist past in the 1960s, because the following generation, invoking the 'blessing of later birth', believed it could manage its relationship to the German past by distancing itself and by moral condemnation. However, the lifting of the taboo on the past, brought about primarily by the students' movement, and the ability to talk about and investigate all the horrors of the past, concealed a much deeper taboo – the taboo on empathizing with those involved and affected, that is, the perpetrators as well as the victims. How profound this taboo is was made plain when a President of the Bundestag was forced to resign from one day to the next, and was consigned to political oblivion, because of a speech.[11] This abrupt event cannot be adequately explained by an inept or offensive use of words. Rather, Philipp Jenninger had expressed empathy with the Germans who had stood passively by during the pogroms of the so-called *Reichskristallnacht* or had applauded them, and he had lent his voice to Heinrich Himmler.

To do justice to the seriousness conferred on one's own life by Auschwitz it is not enough to be indignant about the fact and to distance oneself from it with a declamatory 'Never again'. What is at issue is not only the fact of Auschwitz, but the ability to look its possibility in the face. To do this one must be able to imagine what it meant to be a participant or a victim. Only by opening oneself to the *possibility* of Auschwitz does one become able to shape one's life so that one is forearmed against its becoming a reality. For this to be possible, the frozen block which is Auschwitz must be thawed. And for that, the people who lived at that time must be released from their state as an undifferentiated mass solidified by *rigor mortis*, and made, in a certain sense, comprehensible. This work has been done in part today by the 'children of the perpetrators',[12] and by survivors of the Holocaust.

Let us first picture the situation in which one might have been one of the victims. As a German one usually resists this idea. Does this resistance still contain a residue of the notion of the master race? Perhaps one need only recall that, not too long ago, many people in former Yugoslavia who are now victims would have been unable to imagine such a situation. Whether one is a perpetrator or a victim does not depend on oneself, but on the external constellations of power. But we are not concerned only with genocide and the question whether one belongs to a category of people who traditionally were among the powerful. We are also concerned, for example, with torture, which in certain power formations can be inflicted on anyone.

The first thing to be borne in mind is the possibility that death can be unwitnessed. Probably still more terrible than the death and suffering itself is the fact that under the conditions of modern mass extermination and torture no one bears witness to that death and suffering. The exemplary nature of the death of Socrates, for example, who *bravely* took on himself an unjust verdict, is effaced under the conditions of the twentieth century, for *he* died his death on the stage, as it were, and was able by the manner of it to earn immortal fame. That is not the case with the dead of the twentieth century, who did not die individually but in a mass, or if individually, then unseen and with no one to witness how they bore it. Even though the equation of virtue and happiness is fallacious, nevertheless, it will always make a difference for the person who died *well* – a difference, indeed, of everlasting meaning – *if someone has been looking on*. For only thereby does virtue become real, and is not swallowed up in the vortex of nothingness. This is the 'loneliness of the dying' which threatens us in our period of history, not the average loneliness of the modern person, as understood by Norbert Elias.[13] The question is whether one will be able to maintain one's moral existence when there are no witnesses. The Sophist Antiphon formulated the matter as early as the fifth century BC: 'A man therefore can best conduct himself in harmony with justice, if when in the company of witnesses he uphold the laws, and when alone without witnesses he uphold the edicts of nature.'[14] One of those affected by the Holocaust, Ruth Klüger, whose father died in the gas chambers, expresses the disquiet associated with this situation:

> In their death agony the strong trod on the weak, so that the corpses of the men were always on top, those of the children right at the bottom. Did my father trample on children, on children like me, when he breathed his last? But, after all, he was not someone who used his elbows, and on his first day at school he stood right at the back, leaning against the railing. Does someone who is suffocating reach the limit of freedom and trample on others? Or are there, even then, differences, exceptions?[15]

How did my father conduct himself? asks Ruth Klüger. How would we conduct ourselves? we must ask. The quotation also confronts us with the second question which we must come to terms with in case we become victims. If we hold firmly in mind the terror into which the word Auschwitz sucks us as if into a black hole, and consider it in detail as an everyday reality, as it was experienced by the victims, it emerges that, strictly, there are not only perpetrators and victims but a hierarchy of very fine gradations between them. Perpetrators and victims are terms for poles. But the terrible thing about the National-Socialist extermination system was that these poles were intertwined. That is not meant as an excuse for the perpetrators, but the voices of the victims who tell us that they, too, were perpetrators should be taken seriously. The formula of the identification with the aggressor is known from psychology. There is clear evidence of this in the reports of the persecuted Jews. For example, in his book *Shivitti*, Ka-Tzetnik [concentration camp inmate] 135633 describes a vision in which he saw himself wearing an SS cap.[16] In his book *Wartime Lies*, Louis Begley makes Maciek, the Polish Jewish boy, kill lice 'as the SS kill Jews'.[17] And although Maciek is constantly driven from one hiding place to another by the SS and the Wehrmacht, he plays a game with his tin soldiers in which the brave and orderly SS chase the Russians. Identification with the aggressor is one danger for the victim; the other is collaboration. A problem which has not been fully worked through by the Jewish people is the co-operation of the Jewish councils with the Nazis. The book by Begley just mentioned describes how the Jewish councils lent the Nazis a helping hand in 'selecting' Jews according to categories – anyone who could not prove their identity, who had no work, was below or above a certain age – and arranged for their orderly transportation to the camps.[18] One of the mechanisms of the National-Socialist extermination machinery which ensured that the genocide went so smoothly consisted in constantly making distinctions between the victims. This means that there were always minimally better chances of coming out alive, of distancing oneself from others even in the deepest wretchedness, and sharing in the power of the oppressors even while one was a victim. That is one answer, even if a far from adequate one, to the question why the Jews offered so little resistance to their annihilation. This makes the signal given by the uprising in the Warsaw ghetto all the more significant. More important still are the reports of individuals who were capable of saying 'No' even when it was almost meaningless – even more so if one exposes oneself to the situation of the victim by asking: What would I have done, what would I do? This is the testimony of Ka-Tzetnik 135633:

Because the crematorium was overstretched and the barracks were full to bursting point, the lorries dumped their loads into this ditch, and the SS man turned to the first man he came to in our row and ordered him to take a petrol canister and empty it over the women and children.

'No! No!' he said in Dutch.

> I shall never forget the tormented look of rebellion in his face, and his Dutch 'No!' will always ring in my ears. Never had such a 'No!' been said to a German in Auschwitz.
>
> And while women and children burned, the SS man stamped round behind our row and gave the Dutchman a kick in the backside. Like a piece of dry driftwood his skeleton tumbled into the flames.[19]

Such testimonies may be as remote and untouchable as the fact of the million-fold murder itself. But they do restore their dignity to the victims, by making us realize, in the light of individual events, that the extermination really did take place: on this earth, on particular days, at certain hours and through the actions of individual people, even if there were very many of them. Ethics after Auschwitz poses the question of being-human-well in the light of such testimonies. It will always be the question whether one failed to say 'No' to collaboration with evil – even in situations where it would have cost much less – and still fails to say it.

Now let us consider the situation of the perpetrators. I said that it is difficult for us as Germans to identify ourselves with the victims. But can we really imagine having been the perpetrators, or rather: Are we prepared to face the idea that we could find ourselves in the role of perpetrators? We are prevented from picturing this to ourselves by our pacified, civilized daily life and the belief that it must take terrible criminals to commit such terrible crimes. This casual assumption of the stability of our civilized state might have been shaken in anyone who experienced the innocuous life in former Yugoslavia as a tourist. But Hannah Arendt's book *Eichmann in Jerusalem*[20] has deprived us of the – protective – belief that the dreadful crimes committed at the time of the so-called Third Reich were the deeds of dreadful people. This belief has long prevented us from thinking that these deeds actually concern us. 'I myself' – everyone could say in good faith – 'am not such a dreadful person that I would ever participate in such murders. So what have they to do with me?' Hannah Arendt's book shows that Eichmann was a very simple, somewhat proper, conscientious and far from *evil* man. If only he had been a diabolical demon! The dreadful thing is that Eichmann was like everyone and that everyone could be Eichmann. Hannah Arendt came to her conclusion on the basis of her observations during the Eichmann trial in Jerusalem, and on the basis of the interrogation reports and a partial knowledge of his autobiography. I do not want to give details of his life here; instead, I will quote Hannah Arendt's concluding summary. She speaks of the difficulty the judges had in understanding the accused. Then she goes on:

> Clearly, it was not enough that they [the judges at the Jerusalem trial] did not follow the prosecution in its obviously mistaken description of the accused as a 'perverted sadist', nor would it have been enough if they had gone one step further and shown the inconsistency of the case for the prosecution, in which Mr Hausner wanted to try the most abnormal monster the world had ever seen. . . . The trouble with Eichmann was precisely that so many were like him, and that the many were neither perverted nor sadistic, that they were, and still are, terribly and terrifyingly normal.[21]

In another place she stresses the opinion of a psychiatrist who had examined Eichmann, that 'his whole psychological outlook, his attitude toward his wife and children, mother and father, brothers, sisters, and friends, was "not only normal but most desirable" '.[22]

As the head of Section 4B in Office IV at the headquarters of the Reich security service, Eichmann, this 'normal person', had organized the deportation of the European Jews, that is, ultimately, their transportation to the extermination camps. He claims that he had never hated Jews and had never killed any Jew or non-Jew. He carried out the task assigned to him within the plan for the so-called final solution of the Jewish question with circumspection, energy and bureaucratic punctiliousness. He was thus, operating in a central position, one of those primarily responsible for the annihilation of European Jewry, and was therefore condemned to death by the court in Jerusalem.

Hannah Arendt rightly says that this judgement, and the trial itself, did not solve 'the most serious moral problem presented by the case' or even make it a subject of debate. This problem is that an Everyman took part in and, through his office, actually committed a monstrous crime without even being aware that it was a monstrous crime. That could lead one to conclude that the criminal factor was not the individual at all, but the system. Although there is some truth in this view, and although the monstrousness of the National-Socialist crimes certainly cannot be explained by the actions of individual people alone, this view should not be taken as grounds for *excusing* the individual. Not even Eichmann used this argument to justify himself, although he did point out that in his place eighty million Germans would have acted in exactly the same way. But all he meant by this was that he had *done his duty*.

The moral point is, of course, that neither Eichmann nor anyone else *ought to* have acted as he did. And the question is: What must one be like as a person, which aptitudes must one acquire in order *not* to act like Eichmann, however overwhelming the system of evil may be?

The monstrousness of the Eichmann case and the impression, which is hard to resist, that *evil itself* had taken on an autonomous existence different to the evil actions of human beings, might still prevent us from feeling directly affected by this case. I should therefore like to say something about a psychological investigation which, in a relatively innocuous context, shows the same thing as the Eichmann case: that *everyone*, in certain constellations, is capable of crimes against humanity. I am referring to what is known as the Milgram experiment.[23]

In the early 1960s the American psychologist Stanley Milgram carried out a series of tests to investigate the phenomenon of *obedience to authority*. He summarizes the results as follows:

> This is, perhaps, the most fundamental lesson of our study: ordinary people, simply doing their jobs, and without any particular hostility on their part, can become agents in a terrible destructive process. Moreover, even when the destructive effects of their work become patently clear, and they are asked to carry out actions incompatible with fundamental standards of morality, relatively few people have the resources needed to resist authority. A variety of inhibitions against disobeying authority come into play and successfully keep the person in his place.[24]

The experiment was set up, briefly, as follows: the test subjects – quite ordinary people from the street – were placed in the role of teachers who were to train 'learners' to make certain word associations. They were to bring about this 'learning process' with the aid of a shock generator with which they could subject the 'learners' to electric shocks of 15 to 450 volts. Clearly legible on the shock generator was a scale with the readings: Slight Shock, Moderate Shock, Medium Shock, Powerful Shock, Very Powerful Shock, Danger – Severe Shock.

> The subject was told to administer a shock to the learner each time he gave a wrong response. Moreover – and this is the key command – the subject was instructed to 'move one level higher on the shock generator each time the learner gives a wrong answer.' He was also instructed to announce the voltage level before administering the shock. This served to continually remind the subjects of the increas-

ing intensity of shocks administered to the learner. If the subject reached the 30th shock level (450 volts), he was instructed to continue the procedure using this maximum voltage. After two further trials, the experimenter called a halt to the experiment.[25]

The 'learner', however, was a person initiated into the scientists' intentions, and did not receive real shocks but merely mimed their effects. The screams and convulsions of the 'learner' could be heard and seen by the test subject who had taken over the role of teacher. However, a test subject who hesitated was instructed to continue.

The result varied, depending on the nearness to the victim of the test subject. If the victim was sitting behind a pane of glass covered with a sheet of foil, 65 per cent of test subjects obeyed their orders right up to the most powerful shock of 450 volts. But even when there was acoustic feedback the figure was still 62.5 per cent. To give an impression of the kind of reactions of the victim which were accepted by the test subject, I quote a schematic overview:

> In general, however, the victim indicated no discomfort until the 75-volt shock was administered, at which time there was a little grunt. Similar reactions followed the 90- and 105-volt shocks, and at 120 volts the victim shouted to the experimenter that the shocks were becoming painful. Painful groans were heard on administration of the 135-volt shock, and at 150 volts the victim cried out, 'Experimenter, get me out of here! I won't be in the experiment any more! I refuse to go on!' Cries of this type continued with generally rising intensity, so that at 180 volts his response to the shock was definitely an agonised scream. Throughout, from 150 volts on, he insisted that he be let out of the experiment. At 300 volts the victim shouted in desperation that he would no longer provide answers to the memory test.[26]

Milgram carried out his experiments expressly in relation to the Nazi crimes, and also in the context of the crimes against humanity then being committed by US troops in Vietnam. The matter-of-fact nature of his setting and the arbitrary selection of test subjects prevent us from evading the moral question, by taking flight either into a demonology of evil or into hypotheses about selective careers in the SS. Each of us could have been one of Milgram's test subjects. The question poses itself again: What must one be like, what abilities must one have at one's disposal, to be morally equal to such situations? It clearly is not sufficient to be a decent person with passable moral views – when matters become serious that is not enough.

Hannah Arendt's account and Stanley Milgram's experiments are in the tradition of the Enlightenment: they attempt to acknowledge the reality of evil without at the same time assuming a *power* of evil or a wickedness rooted in the human being. Evil happens. The ethical question consists in what a person must do in order not to be drawn into its vortex.

Although this way of acknowledging evil does result directly from taking seriously the horrors of the twentieth century, the question remains whether it is not, all the same, a naive way. Naivety is something one cannot afford in this context – not when one is concerned with ethics. It must unfortunately be said that an ethics without a concept of evil is worthless in our time. Admittedly, in concerning oneself with this concept one must take account of the fact that to take seriously the horror of evil might well mean to acknowledge its incomprehensibility. Nevertheless, two questions must at least be asked. Firstly, is there something in human beings which meets evil halfway, a tendency towards a joy in evil, which causes them to join in 'the evil which happens'? And secondly, is it adequate to the experience of individuals as a phenomenon to personify the overwhelming power of 'the evil which happens' as a demon or a devil?

Let us begin with the first question. Hannah Arendt's description and Milgram's analysis make it seem plausible that evil could be carried out simply in a technical-bureaucratic way – coolly – without the need for any pleasure, evil intention or sadism on the part of the perpetrator. All we appear to be dealing with here is the highly 'functionizable' nature of the modern transport user and professional person. But even in Eichmann there was also a certain affective involvement, which Hannah Arendt refers to as his unfortunate tendency to show off. For example, he said he was proud to have five million Jews on his conscience. Seen from that standpoint, the image of Eichmann as the conscientious petty bourgeois might appear somewhat different. But we do not have to rely on this example. There are sufficient testimonies to the fact that, within the Nazis' bureaucratic-technical annihilation machinery, participating individuals displayed 'unnecessary' cruelty – if one is allowed to express it thus – and sadistic pleasure. More generally, it can be said that the denigration of Jews as 'subhumans' or non-humans not only made the actions of the perpetrators easier for them, but that the perpetrators – like a large part of the population of the third Reich at the time, incidentally – clearly had an *interest* in this denigration. This interest emerges especially clearly in cases of rape – rape in war and also in quite ordinary, *peaceful* contexts. The degradation of the rape victim, the violation of their humanity, is an important dimension of this type of sexuality – and is, unfortunately, a *principal tendency* of European sexuality in general.[27] Must one assume that a joy in destroying, tormenting, killing is an elementary attribute of the human being? In face of such a question, which cannot be avoided in view of what human beings have inflicted on each other in the twentieth century, even the biblical doctrine of original sin and the Kantian teaching of a radical evil in human beings fall short of the mark. For, according to the Bible story, original sin is partly rebellion against domination, partly curiosity and partly simple violation of a rule – all tendencies which one can readily attribute to human beings without accusing them of fundamental wickedness. And the Kantian concept of radical evil really expresses only the ambivalence of freedom: freedom is always also the freedom to commit evil. Freud, it is true, does speak of a destructive drive. However, the human being postulated by psychoanalysis is always the cultured person, or, let us say rather, the formed person, so that something like a destructive drive can only manifest itself within a certain dynamic constellation of drives, which also depends on external circumstances. The characteristic example, and the most important one in our context, is the unleashing of destructive drive-energies which Freud noted during the First World War. One should think of his writings *Thoughts for the Times on War and Death* and *Civilisation and Its Discontents*.[28] According to these studies the evil in human beings appears as a correlative or, perhaps rather, an outbreak or a reaction against the processes of civilization and culture. In coming to this conclusion Freud clearly struck a balance between his deeply sceptical view of man and his, in principle, enlightened attitude. For the purposes of this ethics, that view of man teaches us that we must all reckon with the fact that under certain conditions something truly evil and malignant can break out in us, a desire for and a joy in degrading, tormenting and destroying others.

I now come to the second question: whether it does justice to the phenomena concerned to refer to 'the evil which happens' as an autonomous power, or as a devil. Here, we must take seriously the fact that the victims, who really had reason to regard the Germans or the SS or the individual SS officer or concentration camp guard as responsible, sometimes did not do so, but spoke explicitly of *the evil*, the devil. I quote from Ka-Tzetnik's book *Shivitti*: 'It is not

Vevke [the cobbler, G.B.] who is rising in the smoke from the crematorium, no – it is he himself, no other than Aschmodai, the King of the Underworld' [trans. E.J. from pp. 60–1].

Philosophy has always made heavy work of acknowledging evil. The reason lies in the basic decision to identify being with virtue, first taken by Plato. After that the bad could never really be conceived as evil, as something in its own right, but only as an absence of the good. Even within Christianity it was not very easy to conceive of evil. Nevertheless, as we know, the personified Devil has existed since the story of the Fall, and remained solidly rooted in cultural history until the eighteenth century. But to conceive of evil was difficult for Christianity, too, especially if one took God seriously as the creator of the universe. Thus, evil was usually regarded as a divine power which had been split off and cast down, as Lucifer. The eighteenth century, whose children we still are, undertook, in the form of the Enlightenment, a grandiose attempt to do away with evil. It turned out, however, to be a largely ideological attempt, in which evil was conjured away in thought rather than in reality. The Devil, experiences of whom were widely reported in the eighteenth century, was unmasked as a *mere figment of the imagination*. The liberation achieved in this way was, however, always illusory, since that which had previously been understood as an imposition, a temptation or an overwhelming power from outside now had to be ascribed to the subject himself. The source of evil was transposed to within, especially to the imagination. The Enlightenment proceeded in a similar way with the evil *in the world*. The *optimism* of the century, which found expression especially in Leibniz's theodicy, disposed of evil by seeing its effects as absorbed into the good in a grand earthly reckoning, or even by regarding it as a mechanism and catalyst of the good. Mandeville's fable of the bees, which teaches that 'private vices' become, or foster, 'public virtues', is a well-known example of this thinking.

In the twentieth century we have lost this trust in the goodness of the whole. Today the certainty of evil is more obvious than that of good. And if we remain true to the Enlightenment at least in not assuming a personalized evil, we still have to come to terms with the experience that evil can be supra-individual, that is, it can take on an autonomous existence *vis-à-vis* the actions of individuals. This possibility that the whole can be the false, as Adorno put it, whether it be the 'system', the state or the social and economic order, must be kept in mind as a basic ethical experience of the twentieth century.

This may indeed be the formula summing up the profound shock to moral confidence which every ethics must now take as its starting-point: *the whole can be the false* – the state can be criminal, the economy exploitative, the conditions of life inhuman. The shattering of moral confidence has made clear the degree to which individual goodness is dependent on the general social and historical conditions in which it seeks to realize itself. I would remind you only of the well-known speech by Heinrich Himmler at the congress of SS group leaders in Poznán on 4 October 1943, in which he praised the morality of the SS men, who had 'endured' the concrete reality of the extirpation of the Jewish people and in so doing, 'aside from exceptional instances of human weakness – had remained decent'.[29] What Himmler was here attempting to associate, as a 'withstanding' of the temptations of human weakness, with the classical virtues of steadfastness, self-mastery and even bravery, is utterly nullified by the context. We can and must say today that to be human well in this situation would have meant precisely *not* enduring what went on around one, and bravery would have been to say 'No' to participation in mass murder. (There are examples of this, too.) One should not conclude from this, however, that virtues such as bravery or a sense of duty were devalued as such through the context of the Third Reich. If one refers to them as mere 'secondary virtues' one needs to state what the primary virtues are. It is true that it depends on the context whether virtues are actually good, that is, form part of being-human-well. But that does not mean that they could be replaced simply by principles as guidance for action.

For even actions guided by principles can be morally nullified by the historical-political context. The use Eichmann made of the categorical imperative may be an example of this.[30] But one would prefer to speak of a *misuse*, as also in the case of Himmler's use of the vocabulary of bravery and the ability of his people to suppress their feelings. But the book by Begley, *Wartime Lies*, already referred to, refutes beyond any doubt the Kantian, i.e. categorical, derivation of the demand for truth. It can be seen that Kant's abstraction from the political-historical context of action was only possible on the basis of *confidence in a moral world order*. For us today, precisely the shattering of this confidence must be the starting-point of ethical reflections.

Basic Moral Ideas

In this section a further attempt will be made to mark out the horizon within which a project for a moral existence can unfold, or against the background of which moral argumentation to establish social regulations can take place. Apart from the civilized state of European man and his historical experience in the last century, certain more or less explicitly basic moral ideas must be considered. By explicit basic moral ideas I refer to ideas anchored in the conventions of human rights and in the German Basic Law. The next section will be devoted to them. Here I am concerned rather with basic moral knowledge, in so far as it is 'tacit knowledge', that is, is passed on mainly implicitly and is manifested only in cases where it is problematized or violated. If this moral background knowledge becomes explicit, it is in the form of concrete notions which imply a command or a prohibition or something worth striving for. Such notions can also be referred to as values. This brings us close to a material ethics of value, as developed by Max Scheler or Nicolai Hartmann.[31] But for us, neither the founding of these values on feeling, as in Scheler, nor their in-itself existence as in Hartmann, can be the guideline. Rather, the basic moral ideas will be taken straightforwardly as a culture which forms the horizon within which moral orientation takes place. Moreover, moral orientation itself, that is, the development of a moral self-awareness or the discourse for establishing social norms, can very well call these basic moral ideas into question. Incidentally, their status as basic moral ideas is in no way affected by the fact that in individual cases they may be violated by concrete actions.

In what follows I shall begin with the basic moral ideas which are so deep-seated that one has reason to suppose that they originate in natural history. They are generally referred to as taboos. Then I shall turn to the basic ideas which stem from the three main sources of our culture, Graeco-Roman antiquity, the Judaeo-Christian religion and, finally, man's great quest for self-determination in the modern period. These latter ideas then lead on naturally to an explication of the basic moral ideas enshrined in the conventions of human rights and in constitutions.

Taboos

Taboos are specific prohibitions which must be strictly observed in a society, on pain of exclusion from that society. They can be so far internalized that their infringement leads to self-punishment, i.e. voluntary exclusion or suicide. This definition is probably too strong to apply to a post-Enlightenment society, especially as violations of taboos in this society have become criminal offences. The result is that, on one hand, rules for atonement within the society have been introduced, and on the other, the individual is no longer permitted to deal with the infringement himself. What is important, however, is that taboos are basic moral ideas which are prior to all social norms. It is therefore, strictly speaking, impossible to formulate what a taboo is, since unconsciousness is an important feature of its status. However, in our culture, they include, at any rate, the taboo on incest and the prohibition on killing other people.

The special status of taboos among the basic moral ideas consists in the immediacy of their effectiveness and the supposition that they may have a pre-cultural origin. The term taboo comes originally from the Polynesian religion, and has been generalized by ethnologists to refer to very strict avoidance-commands or prohibitions on touching which are usually followed unconsciously. Their *incomprehensibility*, and ethnology's original orientation towards primitive cultures, have fostered the view that taboos might be pre-cultural. On the other hand, it has also emerged that taboos are constitutive of culture and society, or, more precisely, that they even define group identities. But this function, too, places them, in a sense, between nature and culture: they may have a basis in nature, but mark precisely the transition to cultural formations. This view is partially supported today by ethology, i.e. the theory on the behaviour of animals. Both aspects, nature and culture, will be elucidated with reference to the examples mentioned, the prohibitions on killing and incest.

Killing a person is not forbidden because it would be a criminal offence. Rather, the killing of a person has been included in the regulations of the penal code so that it can be dealt with within society and does not lead to exclusion from society, blood feuds, etc. One does not abstain from killing because it is a punishable act; clearly, a more deep-seated inhibition is involved. Since, as Konrad Lorenz[32] has shown, species-specific inhibitions on killing exist in the animal kingdom, one might suppose that man, too, is equipped with such inhibitions by his pre-cultural origin. However, the comparison with animals shows that this inhibition on killing can be not only species-specific but group-specific. This is the case with rats, for example. Since, among humans, instances of untrammelled aggression between groups – today we call them 'wars' – can be observed as far back as we can look, only a group-specific inhibition on killing, if any at all, must be assumed among humans. That would mean that the inhibition on killing also marks the start of cultural conditioning, in that it forms group identity by demarcation from what is outside. Konrad Lorenz, who deals with such questions in his book *On Aggression*, inclines to the view that the origin of the prohibition on killing lies in a species-specific inhibition, which later, under cultural conditions, and especially after the invention of weapons, became insufficient.[33]

Whereas no species can survive without a certain form of inhibition on killing its own members, the question of sexual intercourse between close relatives is regulated very differently in different animal species. However, what we call the incest taboo *does exist* among animals. In the case of man, however, it must be said that a society-constituting prohibition is involved. Applied positively, it is the dictate of exogamy, that is, the command that one should seek one's sexual partner in a human group other than one's own. This makes it clear, however, that the incest taboo, or the exogamy command, itself requires cultural elaboration. For it depends on, and helps to define, what is regarded as one's own human group. This implies, moreover, that in some groups or societies an endogamy command can exist, for example, in the caste system, and that, in the Egyptian royal houses, for example, marriage between siblings was quite customary, if not actually demanded. In our society the incest taboo is applied, on a rising and falling scale, between siblings. That, at any rate, is how it has been formulated in law; its extent *qua* taboo cannot be precisely determined.

The non-conventional nature of taboos challenges us to ask about their functions. We have already begun to answer this in speaking of their function in constituting culture or society. Taboos clearly have a function of defining human groups against each other, but also of regulating the relations between these groups. The latter function has been demonstrated especially by Claude Lévi-Strauss in his works on this subject. The most interesting result to emerge from them is the structural similarity between totem clans and the caste system. Totem clans define themselves in terms of a totem, for example, an animal, and observe strict exogamy; that is, their relationships with each other are regulated by an exchange of women. In the caste system this is reversed. In the castes strict endogamy is observed; they therefore see themselves as a natural unit, while they regulate their external relations by exchange of the particular services and products for which they are responsible as a caste.[34]

However, apart from or instead of their social function, a biological or psychological function can be attributed to taboos. As the biological function of the incest taboo, it has long been assumed that *incest* can lead to hereditary defects. According to modern biology, however, that is not a tenable position, except that existing hereditary defects have a greater probability of manifesting themselves from a conjunction of the same genetic material. On the other hand, one can say, of course, that endogamy in a wider or narrower sense could lead to the formation of races and, as a tendency, to a splitting-up of the human species, so that, conversely, all anti-racist arguments and behaviour promote the biological unity of mankind. An evolutionary function of the incest taboo could also lie in the enhancement of variability.

Psychological functions have been attributed to taboos primarily by Sigmund Freud.[35] He believes that they subserve the repression of very fundamental drives. However, this argument has become questionable in view of Bataille's contention that drives grow more violent precisely when they encounter prohibitions.[36]

From an ethical standpoint, all these reflections on the possible functions of taboos are irrelevant, or even dangerous. For example, when Hans Krämer locates the justification for the prohibition on incest 'especially between father and daughter', as he writes,[37] in gene theory, this amounts practically to an ethical suspension of the taboo. Even if hereditary defects, in which Krämer evidently still believes, could appear, they could easily be averted by contraceptives, and nothing would then stand in the way of incest between father and daughter. The ethical significance of taboos lies precisely in the fact that they are *basic moral ideas*, that is, they apply unconditionally. The inhibition stemming from them is pre-rational. Naturally, as an enlightened person one can strengthen oneself or them by clarifying their functional plausibility from case to case. But they would not be what they are if they were really experienced in terms of their possibly specifiable biological, social or psychological functions.

A characteristic feature of the basic moral ideas which we subsume under the heading of taboos is that they are normally obeyed out of intuitive aversion. Every legal elaboration, every cultural restriction or extension of their range of application presupposes their validity in principle. On the basis of the fundamental ban on killing, for example, it is quite possible to suspend this prohibition in typical individual cases. But for this a special legitimation is always needed.

Graeco-Roman basic ideas

So much for taboos. In what follows it will become more difficult to identify basic ideas. In what order should they be presented, and what should be referred to as a basic idea? Let us therefore reflect once more on what such basic ideas are and what they are supposed to achieve: they form a collection of *topoi* in the Aristotelian sense. *Topoi* could best be translated as 'commonplaces', if that were not a pejorative term. *Topoi* are, as it were, stopping-points for rhetoric, common references, ideas which the orator can assume to be shared by his listeners. Moral discourses move within the framework of such *topoi*, using them as reference points. That does not mean, of course, that the basic moral ideas, the *topoi*, are unchanging – but, at any rate, they form the initial starting-point. But these *topoi* also play a part for the individual in projecting his or her moral life. In this case, however, they tend to be the remnants of past forms of living or ideals of humanity, from which one must start out – especially as a young person – if one wants to find out what a moral life can be under the given conditions of life. Here, of course, the decisive thing will be how one comes to terms with the present situation.

I shall take as an example the classical virtue of bravery. This virtue undoubtedly once formed part of being-human-well. But it is easy to see today that it was originally a component of a warlike self-stylization by men. In addition, it was integrated into a moral world order, in the sense that bravery was sure of finding recognition and fame on all sides, among both friend and foe. Even though these marginal conditions have crumbled away today, one will have to deal initially with *topoi* like bravery in one's quest for being-human-well. This is not quite the same as the requirement that one should first abide by what is customary, or the assertion that the moral life only begins beyond customary behaviour. For today the classical virtues, because of their antiquated character, diverge sharply from customary behaviour and are therefore *topoi* which can form the starting-point for a moral life. Imagine, for example, an official in a public authority suddenly getting the idea of being brave.

Let us begin, therefore, with the basic moral ideas of Graeco-Roman origin which can still exert an influence as *topoi*. I should reiterate first of all what I have already said in general terms about the concept of *arete*. Against this background of our moral culture, virtue means to be better, to distinguish oneself from the many, from the common people, from the *unfree*. These are *lordly* virtues in the double sense that they are primarily forms of masculine self-stylization, in particular the self-stylization of the man as warrior, and additionally they are virtues of the *rulers*. However, the *lordly self-confidence* expressed in Graeco-Roman virtues has its precondition and root in self-mastery. Bravery, magnanimity, level-headedness, justice require that one is master of oneself, can set aside one's own wishes, can resist both temptations and demands. Bravery means steadfastness in face of the onset of fear. Magnanimity means being able to disregard one's own interests and allowing others to gain recognition, as well as money. Level-headedness means generally remaining calm and serene in precarious situations and in face of temptations and demands. And, finally, justice is the ability to allow each to receive what is due to him without regard for one's own interests. As a *topos* of moral discourse, justice is the notion of a balance between the divergent interests of the many. For this reason the emblem of justice is the scales. It makes clear that to demand justice does not mean simply to claim one's rights but to see one's rights in relation to those of others.

However, these Graeco-Roman virtues characterize not only the warrior but the independent man within the community, the citizen. The fact that being-human-well was understood to imply independence within the community gave rise to two further moral *topoi*: on one hand respect, especially the mutual respect of citizens for each other's independence, and, on the other, an obligatory bond to the community. At this point we would be inclined to speak of loyalty – but that presupposes a difference between citizen and state. In classical times – in ancient Greece, for example – there was no state as a separate authority; the citizens together formed the state. For this reason the basic value at issue here is referred to in Greek as *politeia*, meaning both the state and the public conduct of the citizens within the state. One could, of course, convey the meaning of this *topos* by the term 'citizen', but that would only make sense if one had in mind a situation in which not everyone was a citizen, so that being a citizen could be regarded as a part of being-human-well. At any rate, in addition to the classical virtues of bravery, magnanimity, level-headedness and justice, we should keep in mind respect, citizenship and community or common welfare as moral reference points or guidelines.

Before attempting to ascertain which *topoi* of our moral culture have come down to us from the Judaeo-Christian religion, I shall briefly consider the question whether there are special basic moral ideas stemming from the Germanic origins of our culture. Because of recent German history, and especially the entanglement of ideas of Germanic origin with National Socialism, this question is difficult to answer today. A value like 'homeland' or 'fatherland' is hardly something one can appeal to nowadays, although this value can be traced back equally well to the Graeco-Roman tradition, to the concept of *patria*. The case may be somewhat different with fidelity. Fidelity is firmness in adhering to a voluntary relationship of allegiance, of the kind which was important in a community dependent on personal bonds, like the system of feudal lords and vassals. It may be that the *topos* of honour also has its origin in this context.

Finally, there is the question whether beauty has a place in this context of basic moral ideas. With regard to the Greek relationship or, better, unity between beauty and virtue one would unquestionably have to answer in the affirmative. There are numerous examples from Greek antiquity demonstrating that mere beauty, that is, beauty of appearance, was regarded as a personal value. Today, beauty certainly could not be invoked as a moral *topos*, any more – incidentally – than obedience.

Basic moral ideas from the Judaeo-Christian religion

If one were asked to list the basic moral ideas originating in the Judaeo-Christian religion, one would think first of the Ten Commandments. But we are now far from invoking the Ten Commandments either in projecting a moral life or in moral argumentation. In a community which has long been structured on secular lines, the Judaeo-Christian religion is no longer a power which can order or organize moral life or moral argumentation. Nevertheless, there are individual *topoi* stemming from the Judaeo-Christian religion which have been assimilated into our secular culture as a kind of

common property. This is especially clear if our culture is compared to those with different religious backgrounds. I would
mention charity and forgiveness as two such *topoi*. The commandment to 'love thy neighbour' is something one can appeal to in its
substance, if not in these exact terms, at any time in our culture.
The demand to help those in need is accepted in principle by
everyone, even if it is not acted upon. The recognition of this
obligation, together with the desire to be relieved of it individually,
has given rise to the large charitable organizations, insurance
systems, the social security net, and so on. It can be seen from this
development that the secularized term for charity is something like
solidarity. The term solidarity, which was the successor to charity
in the workers' movement, freed the preceding term from a defect,
its asymmetry. Solidarity is a reciprocal willingness to help. On
the other hand, it must be said that the Christian commandment
of charity also requires that *solidarity* be exercised towards
strangers. That is the moral of the parable of the Good Samaritan
(Luke 10: 25–37). Solidarity as a reciprocal relationship is always
in danger of being restricted to a circle of friends.[38]

Charity as cultural praxis has given rise in our culture to a
respect in principle for the poor, the weak, the disadvantaged. The
lifting of the slur of inferiority which once attached to sickness and
poverty is no doubt a late consequence of this. Another, earlier
consequence is the virtue of chivalry, which calls for helpful,
magnanimous conduct towards those weaker than oneself,
especially women and children. The general privileging of women
and children in emergencies and situations of violence is derived
from this. Chivalry can be seen as a combination of Graeco-Roman
warrior ideals with Christian charity.

A further important moral *topos* from the Judaeo-Christian
religion is forgiveness, with the associated idea of reconciliation.
That forgiveness and reconciliation are special moral ideas which
have shaped our culture can be seen from the fact that relationships of conflict and guilt can also be resolved by vengeance,
punishment and justice. The Christian idea of reconciliation, originally the reconciliation between God and man, really brought
something new to interpersonal relationships – the possibility of a
new beginning, without a settling of accounts. In Christianity this
idea is emphasized by the notion of the new Adam. Today,
reconciliation and forgiveness are conceptions which influence not
only interpersonal relationships but also criminal law and international relations. These conceptions may, of course, be criticized
on the grounds that the idea of reconciliation is frequently invoked

by the guilty, whereas it is the victims who have to make the effort not to be resentful, to draw a line and to forgo retribution. They do prove, however, that forgiveness and reconciliation are basic conceptions which can be invoked in our culture.

Finally, as a last example of a basic moral idea, I should like to mention the family. The family as a basic value may have originated in ancient Rome, but was raised to an entirely new level by the elevation of marriage to a sacrament within the Christian religion. Despite all the upheavals and disintegrative tendencies besetting the institution, the family has remained a basic idea by which politics and legislation are guided, and which can be made a moral *topos* in projecting a moral life – all the more so the less it forms part of customary behaviour.

Basic moral ideas of the modern age

Finally, let us turn to the basic moral ideas peculiar to the modern age. These basic ideas are closest to us – that is, to our awareness of life and to our real situation as human beings in technical civilization. But in terms of their status they are, in a certain sense, the weakest. The modern basic values spring entirely from the undertaking of European people to construct their own condition and their social circumstances on their own initiative. This is referred to, not incorrectly, as the project of modernity.[39] The basic moral ideas of the modern period correspond to fundamental *topoi* of this project of modernity, and thus have, as a rule, the quality of something explicit and deliberate. These basic values are not, therefore, located diffusely and half-unconsciously somewhere behind us, but are formulated explicitly and are therefore at the boundary of what is canonized as law by the process of social consensus-forming. For this reason, following a discussion of these values, the next section will be concerned with the Declaration of Human Rights and the German Basic Law.

Since the objective of the project of modernity is the self-formation of the human being and his society, *self-determination* is one of the basic values, and perhaps *the* basic value, of the modern period. For the individual, self-determination means, or requires, independence from tutelage, privacy and, in particular, freedom in the choice of religion and way of life. This *topos* is seen as a defensive value acting against influences and external domination and, more generally, as *freedom*; more strictly, with regard both to morality and to legal and political arrangements, it is referred to as *autonomy*. The principle of self-determination, as the self-determination of peoples, naturally contradicts any form of domination and, depending on the group, nation, ethnic grouping or region which espouses it, is of immense explosive power. When formulated as *freedom*, this basic value is more diffuse, but of wider ideological scope. We shall see, however, that in legal norms freedom explicitly takes on a far clearer meaning.

Connected to the basic value of self-determination is the basic value of the individual. The individual is conceived as the subject of self-determination. That the individual asserts his validity as an individual and claims rights on grounds of his particularity and for his particularity, is a typically modern value. Of course, one may surmise that this value is prefigured in the words of the Christian God, 'I have called thee by thy name'. But that each individual human being as such represents and claims an absolute value must be regarded as a specifically modern development.

The progressive realization, or consolidation, of the individual, has given rise in the modern age to two further fundamental values, those of private property and work. The value of private property doubtless has its precursor, too, in the Christian commandment: 'Thou shalt not covet thy neighbour's wife, child, servant, maid, cattle or whatever is his'.[40] But it must be added that the privatization of the commodity sphere is an achievement – if it may be called that – of the modern age. Especially in Europe, feudality and the institution of common land or property, which restricted private property essentially to the house and the reproduction sector, were initially far more powerful institutions for the allocation of goods. Admittedly, the generalization of private property as a principle of goods allocation was prepared for by the development of towns and the rise of the bourgeoisie, that is, of crafts and trade. With the modern age, however, a close relationship between private property and the individual came into being; that is to say, the property sphere was regarded as the objective realization of the person, and therefore was accorded the same dignity as the individual himself.

However, because this form of social realization could not be generalized – it did not enable the workers and the poor to secure social status as persons – the social value attached to work was progressively heightened. Since antiquity, work had not represented a value in European culture, but had been seen as something which, while necessary, did not form part of being-human-well. As far as possible, it was delegated to others, i.e. slaves and dependants. By contrast, the valorization of work since the early modern period, and its function in securing social status for *everyone*, is one of the most important developments of moral culture. This can be seen indirectly today in the threat posed in principle to our social identity and the moral-political order by the fact that society is running out of work.

Tolerance is a further basic value of the modern period. It, too, is related to the basic value of self-determination. Tolerance is the requirement that one concede to others the same self-determination which one claims for oneself. In that one's own self-determination is linked to claims to the truth and validity of, for example, one's own moral guidelines or one's own views, tolerance towards others retroactively influences one's own person. For if one regards as possible and approves in others different value guidelines and different *truths* to one's own, that means, in principle, that one is calling one's own into question. There is a very fine depiction of this reciprocal effect in Gotthold Ephraim Lessing's drama *Nathan the Wise* (1779), where the relationship of tolerance between the religions of Christianity, Judaism and Islam is interpreted in such a way that none of the religions can know whether it is the true one. The true ring has been lost. This already indicates that tolerance is a value which regulates the relations not only between persons but also between social groups, especially groups defined by their world views and groups from different cultures. How difficult it is in practice to accept the impact of tolerance on one's own person or group, and therefore to question the validity of one's own claims, must be clear.

In conclusion, I would like to discuss two further basic values of the modern period, which are also correlatives of each other: rationality and nature. Rationality is very closely bound up with the project of modernity, in that this principle demands the reconstruction of the given reality according to freely chosen principles. It calls for rationality of government, rationalization of the economy, rational religion or, as Kant put it, 'religion within the limits of reason alone'. All these are projects of the Enlightenment, projects which entail consciously appropriating, reconstructing and subjecting to criteria of legitimacy everything which was originally given and handed down by tradition and revelation, or by the facts of history. Accordingly, to be rational, to conduct one's life rationally, are the basic values of modern self-awareness. In the context of Enlightenment philosophy, *rationality* is nothing less than the basic *topos* of being-human-well. We have seen that Max

Weber was able to regard the principle of rationalization as the prime characteristic of modern developments.

The value attached in the modern period to nature exists in a certain contraposition to this basic value of rationality. Previously, especially in the Christian-dominated West, nature as such had not been a value. It only became one in the eighteenth century, when the first doubts about the project of modernity were beginning to arise. Nature was now understood as the given, the original, something not made by men, which was good for precisely that reason. In evaluating nature in this way, critics of modernity were able to hark back to certain notions of the ancient world, by which, since the Greek school of Sophists, nature had been contrasted to culture, human law and convention. Nature could thus act as a counter-authority and a critical principle *vis-à-vis* the human project. A natural mode of life, natural law, primitive peoples close to nature, natural healing methods – all these are criteria against which modernity's basic values of self-determination and self-formation have been problematized. As Habermas has argued in his book *The Philosophical Discourse of Modernity*,[41] this self-problematization has accompanied the project of modernity since its early stage. As this project of modernity has now, under the conditions of technical civilization, entered a crisis, it is understandable that special importance is currently attached to the value of nature. But as nature is very closely bound up with other modern values, it, too, as we shall see, is itself caught up in this crisis.

Human Rights, Fundamental Rights

Human rights and fundamental rights as themes of moral discourses

The discussion of human rights, as set down in the Universal Declaration of Human Rights[42] and the European Convention of Human Rights,[43] and of the fundamental rights formulated in the Basic Law of the Federal Republic of Germany,[44] has its place in ethics as the horizon of moral discourses. In these discourses a considerable number of further themes which can serve as starting-points for moral argumentation are identified, and these themes have a special character. Moral discourses, as we know, are concerned with establishing conventions for regulating social actions, whether these conventions are customs or positive laws. Now, human rights and fundamental rights are themselves such conventions, which are enshrined as positive law. If further conventions are then agreed for purposes of legislation, issues concerning their relationship to human rights or fundamental rights might be concerned merely with conformity – for example, whether a new law conforms to the constitution. Verification of this would not be described as moral discourse. All the same, such verification is not a purely juristic discourse. It must be noted, to begin with, that while the Basic Law and the European Convention of Human Rights have the status of law in the Federal Republic, universal human rights do not, since the Basic Law merely *declares its recognition* of the latter.[45] But even this difference is not decisive, especially as much of the content of the universal human rights is contained in the European Convention of Human Rights.[46] Rather, it must be said that general moral themes are addressed in the formulations of human rights and fundamental rights, and that while these are essentially enclosed within a formal legal framework for our society, their substance is by no means exhausted by this form of expression. This applies to concepts such as dignity, life, education, work, freedom. When used as terms in formulations of fundamental rights, these concepts *also* contain an element of surplus meaning, namely a moral potential. In any new social convention which makes reference to these themes, this moral potential is invoked, interpreted and given content. The indeterminacy and undefined nature of these themes as they appear in human and fundamental rights is crucial for their hybrid status between morality and law. But it is reference to them which really makes discourses into moral ones, since matters within these discourses then become *serious* – serious for the society in which we live. Whether or not they are respected, and the content they are given, continuously define the kind of society in which we live.

Human rights and fundamental rights play only a minor role in projecting a moral existence. However, there are people who commit themselves to human rights and fundamental rights to an exceptional degree, and realize their moral existence in so doing. This applies, for example, to workers for Amnesty International. In themselves, human and fundamental rights tend, by and large, to be neutral with regard to a moral life. That is a fact, which is to say that it could also be otherwise. The reason is that human rights and fundamental rights are *liberal* rights, which, consequently, do not demand anything of the individual, but secure his autonomy and self-determination. Historically, human rights have come into being essentially as defensive rights against an over-mighty state – for example, the Declaration of Human Rights (1789) against the absolutist state, and the Universal Declaration of Human Rights of 1948 against totalitarian states. This was different in countries which had set up a certain form of living as the state goal, as in the case of socialism in the former German Democratic Republic. Its constitution[47] contained the principle: 'Work with us, plan with us, govern with us!' (Art. 21, §1). At any rate, human rights and fundamental rights provide a very wide framework for the projecting of a moral life, within which – or possibly against which – one can define one's moral existence. In the Federal Republic of Germany this framework is referred to as the 'free, democratic, basic order'. Still more generally, it can be characterized as that of a constitutional community; that is to say that a moral life is conceived against the background of a convention by which the people with whom one lives have decided from the first to live in a constitutional community.

The Constitutional community

The term 'constitutional community' is not an expression of the Convention of Human Rights or the Basic Law. But it refers to the basic structure of the society which is defined by the existence of these conventions. Such societies are communities which regulate their communal life solely through conventions and, in particular, through those which can be made permanent as laws and are thus independent of support by individual members of the society. That this is a special social situation can be seen, for example, from the fact that in a feudal system there can be *laws* which are privileges conferred individually by the king. Laws, therefore, are permanently established conventions which are neutral towards persons. A further characteristic is that they can be *sanctioned*, that is, their infringement can be punished and their observance enforced by law. It is clear that this implicitly presupposes an agency to which appeals can be addressed and which is responsible for sanctioning, that is, a judicial and executive agency – meaning a state. In practice human rights and basic law presuppose this state, or themselves define the conventions on which it is based, and the legitimacy with which it is endowed. Both the Universal Declaration of Human Rights and the European Convention of Human Rights, as well, of course, as the Basic Law of the Federal Republic of Germany, define this state as a democracy. One might see a problem in this, and regard it historically as an effect of the dominance of western democracies in the formulation of human rights at the United Nations. But this problem impinges, rather, on the universal validity of human rights. To the extent that we regard human rights as reference points for moral argumentation with the aim of establishing regulations in *our* society, we are unaffected by these problems. For within our society moral argumentation takes place against the horizon of a fundamental decision in favour of democracy.

Democracy

The basic decision to live together in a constitutional community, i.e. a society the life of which is regulated by permanent conventions, implies a number of moral values which are made explicit in human or fundamental rights. This is the point at which the outcome of discursive ethics can be incorporated in the reality of moral discourses. Discursive ethics, as developed, in particular, by Karl-Otto Apel, has demonstrated that to enter into moral discourse implies certain values, such as the reciprocal *recognition* of the persons participating in the discourse, and their *equality*, in that the relevance of their contributions to the discourse depends only on their argumentative content, and not on the social position of the person expounding them.[48] The transition from such a counter-factual discursive ethics, applicable to an ideal discourse free of domination, to real social discourses which contribute to the formation of social conventions, has been attempted by Habermas.[49] Without an element of positive law, that is, without the conventional rights of participation and equality, of the kind which operate in democracy, this transition cannot be made.

The principle of democracy is defined, on one hand, by establishing the origin of state authority and, on the other, by the rights of participation of the individual member of society. Since the Basic Law is a *constitution*, the origin of state authority can be directly formulated. In the human rights which, in the version of the Declaration of Human Rights of 1948, are always introduced by the formula: 'Everyone . . .', the question of the origin of state authority is even subordinated to the rights of participation. I quote Article 21 of the Universal Declaration of Human Rights of 1948:

1 Everyone has the right to take part in the government of his country, directly or through freely chosen representatives.
2 Everyone has the right to equal access to public service in his country.
3 The will of the people shall be the basis of the authority of government; this will shall be expressed in periodic and genuine elections which shall be by universal and equal suffrage and shall be held by secret vote or by equivalent free voting procedures.

In these terms the rights of participation and the equality of each individual are formulated. The principle of the division of powers, which is equally essential to our conception of democracy, is not contained in the formulation of human rights, so that they do not express so clearly that the rights of participation relate in particular to what we call *moral discourse on conventions for regulating social behaviour*. This is contained, however, in the formulation of Article 20, Paragraph 2 of the Basic Law: 'All state authority emanates from the people. It is exercised by the people by means of elections and voting and by separate legislative, executive and judicial organs' [trans. E.J.]. Moreover, in the Basic Law the principle of democracy is combined with the right of resistance. Paragraph 4 of Article 20 states: 'All Germans shall have the right to resist any person seeking to abolish this constitutional order, should no other remedy be possible' [trans. E.J.].

Although this right of resistance has a long history, it was adopted in the German Basic Law, as already mentioned, in the light of the experiences of the so-called Third Reich. Legal scholars claim that in practical terms it is rather ineffective or even superfluous, because the details of the Basic Democratic Order contain sufficient internal possibilities of revision regarding the formation of resistance, complaints about the constitution, or even the possibility of modifying the Basic Law, in any case.[50] For the consciousness of the individual, however, the right of resistance is of extraordinary significance. It implies that everyone has the right critically to monitor the observance of the fundamental rights, and that, in principle, the political sovereignty of the individual remains revocable. For in the concrete political context the formulation that all power emanates from the people is somewhat illusory, since in practice it is always delegated to the organs of state. But the right of resistance implies that this delegated sovereignty is in principle revocable by the individual. The right of resistance is therefore the right of the individual to check the conduct of the organs of state in terms of general principles, in particular human rights, and to engage in civil disobedience in particular cases.

Human dignity

The concept of human dignity is the central and undefined basic concept both of the Basic Law and of the 1948 Declaration of Human Rights. Article 1, Paragraph 1 of the Basic Law is as follows: 'The dignity of man is inviolable. To respect and protect it is the duty of all state authority' [trans. E.J.]. Here, then, the first function of the state is stated to be the protection of human dignity. Only after this, in Paragraph 2 of Article 1, is there mention of human rights. This structure is found in exactly the same form in the Declaration of Human Rights, in its preamble, which begins: '*Whereas* recognition of the inherent dignity and of the equal and inalienable rights of all members of the human family is the foundation of freedom, justice and peace in the world.' Here, too, the dignity of the human being is placed ahead of his or her rights and referred to as the foundation of the latter. But what actually is dignity?

It can be said, of course, that the basic or human rights which are then listed constitute the dignity of man. This view is not entirely wrong. But if the basic or human rights are understood to be the explication of what is contained in the concept of human dignity, that assumes that this concept or, perhaps one should rather say, this *idea* is itself richer and capable of further explication. Strictly speaking, the basic and human rights are put in place to *protect* human dignity. They are not that dignity itself.

The term dignity [German: *Würde*] means worth or value, but a value which is socially recognized. If one tried to make this formulation into a definition it would certainly be inadequate, as it would not contain the force of the idea of dignity. *Dignity* calls for respect and distance. The connotations of the term, and many of its usages, imply someone in an elevated position who acts with dignity, is of high rank [*Würde*]; indeed, the expression conjures up a numinous quality, an aura of holiness floating around the bearer of dignity. The wording of Article 1 of the Basic Law is actually very peculiar, in saying that the dignity of man is 'inviolable'. This expression brings dignity into the proximity of a taboo. The impression is further reinforced by the assertory diction. The

Article does not state that the dignity of the human being *should not* be violated – although that is certainly also meant; it confers on it the status of something untouchable. Such diction is fully appropriate to a text which, as we have maintained, represents a transition from morality to law. The *dignity of man* is a moral *topos* which acts as a guideline for the formulation of basic human rights.

The connotations of the elevated and holy which we associate with the concept of dignity also give the first clause of the Basic Law a rather radically democratic and secular meaning. The lofty and sacred status which worshippers earlier were prepared to confer on particular people or beings is now accorded to *every* human being as a human being. One should treat every human being with respect, and feel some ultimate awe in one's dealings with him or her. In this we undoubtedly find once more the mutual respect of citizens which we encountered earlier as a classical *topos*, together with the absolute value which the modern age assigns to the individual. It is important to note, however, that human beings are referred to here simply as human beings, and not as citizens or in terms of some other relationship, and that the respect to be paid them is not directed at anything definite in or about them, such as their reason (as in the Kantian realm of rational beings); nor is it required that their special quality should manifest itself in any way. The dignity of human beings forms part of their humanity as such.

'The human being' is thus the second undefined and indeterminate concept in the German Basic Law. The recipient or bearer of the fundamental rights continues to be general and indeterminate – in expressions such as 'everyone has the right' or 'all persons are' – until Article 8 (freedom of assembly), which refers to 'all Germans'. By contrast, it is characteristic of the Declaration of Human Rights that each article begins either with 'everyone' or 'no one' or 'all human beings'. What constitutes being human is thus left just as open as what constitutes dignity. All the same, the formulation of the Declaration of Human Rights does make a fundamental statement when, in the Preamble, it speaks of 'all members of the human family'. Of course, the term 'family' is used here in an extended and metaphorical sense, but it does refer to 'all human beings' as a group defined extensively by relationships of kinship: one is a human being in that one belongs through relationships of kinship to the 'family of man'. This form of words, which, of course, is also crucial to the recognition of human rights in the Basic Law, contains important implications – important, precisely, for moral discourses. For, according to it, to be a human being is not defined by the possession of certain powers or endowments, such as language or reflection or consciousness or the like; rather, one is a human being by virtue of birth: one is born a human being. This conception is further reinforced in Article 1 of the Declaration of Human Rights, at least in its first sentence, which is as follows: 'All people are born free and equal in dignity and rights.' Admittedly, this morally far-reaching formulation is straight away withdrawn, not to say ruined, in the second sentence of the Article, which states: 'They are endowed with reason and conscience and should act towards one another in a spirit of brotherhood.' Reading this, one will prefer the wording of the Basic Law, which leaves the term 'human being' entirely undefined and indeterminate. With regard to the question of the disabled, and the debate on abortion, the formulation in the Declaration of Human Rights deprives these rights of their moral basis. For neither can it be said of all people that they are endowed with reason and conscience, nor is it advisable to make the state of being human start at birth. Altogether, the formulation of Article 1 seems to conflict with the intuition of the Preamble. For people yet unborn could, of course, be seen as part of the 'family of man'. Equally, through ideas of science fiction, which are probably only anticipations of the future, one is now sufficiently familiar with the idea that beings might exist who are endowed with reason and conscience, and perhaps even with a sentient heart, but are not members of the 'family of man'. And these beings – as was the case with Frankenstein's monster – also lay claim to dignity.

What can we learn from this minimal engagement with arguments concerning human rights? This much, at any rate: that it is important that their basic concepts be indeterminate, and any attempt to give them positive content as individual rights can, when measured against the original intention, prove inadequate. That does not mean, however, that in moral argumentation one should not start out from positively formulated human rights. For the recognition and assertion of these is already difficult enough. But it can be seen that the conventions enshrined in them do need to be developed further through moral discourse, and must be constantly reformulated in the light of new problems which arise historically. Since the Basic Law sketches the basic outlines of our social conception of ourselves, and human rights the basic outlines of our human conception of ourselves, precisely the questions which take issue with these basic outlines prove to be moral questions. Through them the questions as to how we conceive of ourselves as human beings, and of our society as a society, become a serious matter.

Rights of freedom

Let us turn now to the actual basic or human rights. Here, again, it should be noted that what is of interest from the moral standpoint is always the undefined content of these rights, whereas their establishment as law represents the permanent form given to the consensus regarding the moral *topos* in question. Moreover, their formulation as law is, as such, a specification of the consensus, in that a law articulates a claim which is in principle enforceable. The concept of law presupposes an authority before which these claims can be asserted – a judge. But a judge alone would be of no use if nothing resulted from his verdict – that is to say that an executive power is also needed. Thus, in embryo, we already have the state. Now, with regard to the Basic Law it is not surprising that the state is an integrating partner of the fundamental rights, since the Basic Law is, after all, a constitution. As far as human rights are concerned, they simply presuppose the factual existence of states throughout the world and formulate, in particular, which rights human beings should have *vis-à-vis* these states. It follows from this that one has already decided in favour of or presupposed the state in participating in the formulation of basic moral consensuses as laws. All the same, the state remains a fact and cannot be morally legitimized.[51]

That the state is a correlative both of fundamental rights and of human rights can also be derived from its historical origin in the course of the French Revolution. Human rights were formulated as rights of emancipation from the state.[52] In general, fundamental rights or human rights are divided into rights of freedom and social rights, to which I would add 'safeguarded goods' as a third area. Rights of freedom are essentially defensive rights *vis-à-vis* the state, social rights are demands on the state to establish certain conditions of life, and safeguarded goods are demands that the state *preserve* certain given circumstances and possibilities of human beings.

First of all, the rights of freedom. Of them it is true to an exceptional degree that they are defined in relation to the state or, more generally, the community; they are defensive rights against interventions from outside. The fundamental rights of the Basic Law are largely rights of freedom. Social rights, which take up a large amount of space in the Declaration of Human Rights, are not so firmly anchored in the Basic Law. I shall list a number of rights of freedom. The Basic Law guarantees:

- the free development of personality (Art. 2);
- freedom of religion (Art. 4);
- of occupation (Art. 12);
- of movement (Art. 11);
- of expression (Art. 5, §1);
- of science and art, research and teaching (Art. 5, §3);
- of assembly and association (Arts 8, 9).

In these rights of freedom a large number of possible activities of the individual are protected from state intervention. Whether the individual wants to be active in these ways is left open, or it is assumed that the individual is such that these fields and the scope of freedom they call for are important. With regard to moral discourse it can be said that the headings of the various dimensions of freedom are moral *topoi*. They designate fields or possible activities which are essential to the individual's – or, better, the citizen's – conception of himself. For each of them is a field of activity in which individuals create for themselves a *public* reality. That is especially clear in the case of freedom of expression. Article 5 does not state that everyone can have an opinion, but that they have the right to express it: 'Everyone has the right freely to express and to disseminate his opinion by speech, writing and pictures and freely to inform himself from generally accessible sources' [trans. E.J.]. It might be different in the case of freedom of religion. Article 4, Paragraph 1 states: 'Freedom of faith and of conscience, and freedom of creed, religious or ideological, are inviolable' [trans. E.J.]. Freedom here is indeed the freedom to have a faith of one's own. This becomes especially clear in the case of conscience. For conscience, or freedom of conscience, means that the individual is granted an ultimate preserve in which he or she remains outside state instruction and obligations. That this is not intended merely in the sense that 'thoughts are free' is demonstrated by Paragraph 3 of Article 4: 'No one may be compelled against his conscience to render war service as an armed combatant' [trans. E.J.]. It should be noted, however, that Article 4, i.e. the freedom of belief and religion, defines not merely a right of freedom but a good to be safeguarded as well. Hence, the term 'inviolable' appears again here.

Taken together, the rights of freedom define the dimensions in which the civic individual seeks to express and develop himself publicly, but without the state. In this regard Article 2 is both a summary and a general heading for these rights of freedom: 'Everyone has the right to the free development of his personality in so far as he does not violate the rights of others or offend against the constitutional order or the moral code' [trans. E.J.]. It should be noted that this first paragraph of Article 2 does not define a right to education, which would not be a right of freedom but a social right. It appears under human rights, but not under fundamental rights. Rather, the right of free development of the personality is the liberal principle by which the citizens secured a *state-free* public sphere, that is, society as distinct from the state. This can be seen particularly vividly in Article 12 (free choice of occupation). Here, the freedom in the choice of occupation of Paragraph 1 is combined with protection from obligatory and compulsory work in Paragraphs 2 and 3. In this way the whole sphere of work is made dependent on relationships of social contract. In this, incidentally, one can also discern the historical origin of the basic and human rights, in the struggle for liberation from socage, feudality and serfdom.

It remains to be noted that the rights of freedom contain moral *topoi* which delineate our conception of the social existence of an individual. Any modification of these rights would be a moral question, since it would require a redefinition of this conception of ourselves; any need to refer to one of these dimensions or *topoi* shows that one has touched on a question through which matters become serious, in that this conception of ourselves has been affected.

Social rights

As mentioned earlier, social rights are less prominent in the Basic Law than in the Universal Declaration of Human Rights. The reason, undoubtedly, is that the Declaration of Human Rights *costs nothing*; while it formulates goals and desirable ends, it provides no means of enforcing them before an authority. That would be different if they were adopted in the catalogue of fundamental rights. According to the Declaration of Human Rights, there exists a right to work (Art. 23), a right to social security (Art. 22), a right to education (Art. 26) and even a right to a certain standard of living. Article 25 states:

LIVERPOOL
JOHN MOORES UNIVERSITY
AVRIL ROBARTS LRC
TEL. 0151 231 4022

Everyone has the right to a standard of living adequate for the health and well-being of himself and of his family, including food, clothing, housing and medical care and necessary social services, and the right to security in the event of unemployment, sickness, disability, widowhood, old age or other lack of livelihood in circumstances beyond his control.

(This right to an appropriate standard of living was again underlined in Article 11 of the 1966 Convention of Human Rights of the United Nations.) Of these social rights only the right to education has legal validity, as mediated through the European Convention of Human Rights.[53] Most of the others are contained in the European Social Charter, which, however, is only a political declaration of intent, and is not legally binding on the contracting parties.

It is not at all surprising that states, especially those which regard themselves as liberal, do not include social rights in their fundamental rights. For in so doing they would impose on themselves material obligations in favour of the individual. But from a moral standpoint, social rights, for which the Basic Law at least *declares its support*, carry the same weight as the rights of freedom. For they, too, embody contents on the value of which a social consensus can be assumed to exist. Even though they cannot be regarded as fundamental rights in the German Federal Republic, but merely as human rights, they are nevertheless *topoi* which can be used as starting-points, or reference points, in argumentation about specific social regulations, and particularly laws. Although violation of them – as when our state does *not* have employment available for everyone – does not call our social conception of ourselves into question (since the Federal Republic regards itself as a liberal society), nevertheless, moral indignation is certainly legitimate, and an appeal to the human right to work politically effective. The case was, or is, different in socialist states, which guaranteed, or guarantee, a legal right to work. Thus, Article 24 of the constitution of the GDR stated: 'Every citizen of the German Democratic Republic has the right to work. He has the right to employment and free choice of employment in keeping with social requirements and his personal qualifications' [trans. E.J.]. But, of course, the GDR did not regard itself as a liberal society, but as a socialist one.

Safeguarded goods

I come, finally, to what I have referred to as 'safeguarded goods'. These are values, possibilities or qualities with which human beings are assumed to be endowed by nature, so that their formulation as rights by the state requires that the state provide arrangements for safeguarding them. A considerable number of such safeguarded goods are contained in the Basic Law. Foremost among them is the right to life. Article 1, Paragraph 2 reads: 'Everyone has the right to life and to inviolability of his person. The freedom of the individual is inviolable' [trans. E.J.]. Every possible recipient or holder of fundamental rights does, of course, *live*, so that no special quality can be ascribed to him by these words. The aim of the article is to formulate life itself as a good worthy to be preserved and protected. This formulation might be regarded as the liberal version of social rights, for a number of measures to safeguard the individual's right to life could, indeed, be expected of the state. In the second part of the paragraph freedom appears as a substantial good. Here, too, a great deal could be demanded of the state if one expects it not only to respect the rights of freedom but to protect the individual from curtailment of his freedom. The qualifying statement in Paragraph 2 shows that, here too, freedom is understood in the liberal sense. For it states: 'These rights may only be encroached upon pursuant to a law' [trans. E.J.]. By comparing this, in particular, with Article 2 of the European Convention of Human Rights, it becomes clear that both life and freedom are understood here as substantial goods in that they can only be *withdrawn* on grounds of legitimized executive measures by the state.

The other safeguarded goods are secrecy of postal and telephonic communications, inviolability of dwellings, security, the family, property and recently, according to Article 20a of the Basic Law, the *natural foundations of life*. We recognize here a number of modern basic values such as privacy, property and nature. The right to security means, of course, outward security, but also, above all, legal security. On this point both the Declaration of Human Rights and the European Convention contain a good number of basic provisions which are intended to ensure security for the individual in legal proceedings, and to protect him against degrading punishments. According to Article 6 the family, through its origin a Roman and Christian basic value, is placed under the special protection of the state order. The Declaration of Human Rights describes the family as 'the natural and fundamental group unit of society' (Art. 16, §3). With regard, above all, to the *topoi* of the family and nature it becomes clear that these basic values are regarded in the Declaration as responsibilities of the state. It is the function of the state to protect the natural foundations of life and property, to safeguard legal and outward security and to guarantee the inviolability of dwellings and of postal and telephonic secrecy.

Here too, in the safeguarded goods, we are dealing with *topoi* which specify goods which are essential to people's conception of themselves. However, they are not actually *topoi* of one's *moral* conception of oneself, but rather, in a sense, the preconditions of that conception. 'Grub first, then morals', says Bertolt Brecht. But they are inalienable prerequisites of a life fit for human beings. Moral theoreticians who do not elaborate the morality of the individual in terms of being-human-well, as I have done here, but interpret it rather in the Aristotelian sense of the 'good life', have accordingly paid most attention to this area of what I have called safeguarded goods. In particular, Martha Nussbaum[54] has attempted to draw up a catalogue of basic goods. This is, of course, of the highest importance because, from the standpoint of humane politics, a primary concern must be to create the preconditions of a life fit for human beings in the first place. It is therefore right that they, together with social rights, should take up a large amount of space in the Declaration of Human Rights. But, to stress the point once more, their realization is not a moral question, but a political and, in some cases, an economic one.

I now arrive at my conclusion. Fundamental rights and human rights mark out the near horizon for moral discourses. Basic and human rights are the most important of the *topoi* which can serve as guidelines for conventions for the regulation of social conduct, but are often also the most fragile. Just because they have already been formulated as rights, they can easily be called into question, and can be changed by explicit conventions. On the other hand, although their content is in most cases vague, so that they contain a moral potential going beyond their wording, their wording itself makes them *something which can be readily grasped*. More long-standing and fundamental moral conceptions than the fundamental rights may exist in our society, but it is difficult to appeal to them since they are not explicitly formulated. By contrast, it can be assumed that fundamental rights and human rights are acknowledged by everyone in our society. That they, too, are alterable and in need of revision will emerge, precisely, from moral discourses.

Newly arising historical problems which bring with them a need for regulation, or a widening of the horizon through contact and coexistence with other cultures, enforce revisions which also affect human rights. For, as we have seen again and again, these human rights, despite their universal claims, are very strongly influenced by European culture and history.

— 3 —

The Moral Life

Skills for Moral Living

Having sketched the horizon within which, today, a moral existence must be defined, and moral argumentation conducted, we shall now turn to the question as to what constitutes the moral life itself. What expectations are aroused by this question, and what guidance on moral living can be expected from a written text? In a previous chapter I wrote that, for the individual, a question should be regarded as moral if it decides what kind of a person he or she is. Moral questions are those through which matters become serious for the individual. Now, one will not expect to come upon this seriousness while reading a text, and still less will a text decide what kind of person the reader is. The most that can be indicated in a book is the dimensions by which a moral existence can be defined for the individual today, against the background of our history and the current situation of human beings. The medium of written communication cannot enable us to anticipate when matters will become serious for an individual, and, in particular, they cannot equip the individual human being with the aptitudes needed to confront that seriousness. If such aptitudes for moral living are to be acquired, a text can, at most, indicate types of practices through which one can hope to acquire them. In my attempt to meet these expectations, this section of the chapter will sketch only the initial leap which must be taken when embarking on a moral life, while the next will deal with the question of what it means, under given conditions, to be human well; the third, finally, will set out in more detail what is involved when matters become serious for someone.

First of all, however, I shall sum up what has already been said, to make clear the basis from which the initial leap must be made, and the obstacles a moral existence must overcome.

The description of the situation of the modern human being, our own situation, turned out to be somewhat sceptical from the moral point of view. More precisely, it emerged that morality is superfluous in the average life situation. Everyday behaviour is sufficiently regulated by customary practices, and as these practices are group- and system-specific, they extend into every corner of existence. The fields of public action are differentiated into instrumental subsystems, so that the system-imperatives of these subsystems are sufficient as guidelines for actions, right down to the actions of individual firms and authorities. Actions are organized instrumentally in terms of system goals, and the means adopted to attain them require, above all, behaviour conforming to the system. What is left over – the sphere of personal biography and private existence – is largely taken over from individuals by experts. The individuals' relationship to them, whether it is one of trust or of dependence, relieves them of the necessity of constructing a way of life of their own. And as for the other pole, the great whole, society and the state, it is shaped by liberal principles and does not call for any commitment from the individual. The interplay of the interests pursued by individuals and groups – so the basic liberal assumption runs – will doubtless work out for the common good (with a little guidance if necessary). Morality is not required.

And yet, as we have seen, moral questions *do exist*. There are biographical constellations, there are developments and situations, which decide what kind of people we are. How are we to recognize them, and how must we be prepared to meet them? In addition, historical experience teaches us that one can find oneself in situations in which, by following customary practices, by remaining discreet and performing the required services on the basis of one's functional competence, one can incur guilt. How must we forearm ourselves to be able to break out of such situations, should it be necessary? In these questions there is no help from outside. Looking ahead, we can assume neither that the whole will be good, nor that virtue will be successful. Our moral confidence in the world has been profoundly shaken by the experiences of the last century.

All this means that morality today begins with scepticism. In a state of civilization in which both the individual and society are largely relieved of the burden of moral questions, but in which the questions as to what the individual is as a human being, and what the society is as a society, are nevertheless posed, moral existence must see itself as a springing away from what already exists, a new departure. The desire for a moral life is linked, strange as that may sound, with the Greek idea of *arete*, according to which virtue means: to be better. Today, too, a moral life requires that one be different, better than the many, that one break away from what merely happens. Morality begins with resistance.[1]

Selfhood

The break-out into a moral life is, first of all, a journey into *selfhood*. Ernst Tugendhat, who rightly observes that there are not only reasons but also motives for a moral life, sums up these motives as an initial decision to be a good human being. But that says both too much and too little. It says too much because the only certain thing in a break-out is what one is leaving behind, not any possible goal of virtue. And it says too little in that Tugendhat defines the good human being as a co-operative partner.[2] But one is already a co-operative partner by virtue of adhering to customary practices, and conforming functionally to systems. All that is not the goal of morality but its precondition, and it can also be assumed to apply to any average modern person. Undoubtedly, these premises are not innate but are acquired, both by the individual and by the European human being in general, through hard training and profound socialization. But morality only begins when one is able to break through customary behaviour, and that requires practice.

To illustrate this I shall give two surprising and, from the point of view of cultural history, revealing examples. One comes from the book by Ruth Klüger already mentioned, *Weiter leben. Eine Jugend.* As a twelve-year-old girl Ruth Klüger was imprisoned in a concentration camp. When a selection was made in the women's camp to segregate women between the ages of fifteen and forty-five for a labour camp – and labour meant, at least, continuing to live – the girl had difficulty in giving an age other than her true one. When she had already been rejected, which would have meant her certain death, her mother begged her to try again with another SS selection officer, giving an incorrect age. She then resolved to claim that she was already thirteen! Only when a female guard assisting the SS man whispered to her that she should say she was fifteen did she actually do so.[3]

The second example is from Mark Twain's famous novel *Huckle-*

berry Finn. Huck, the son of an asocial drinker, teams up with the escaped Negro slave Jim, and they both want to reach a state in which slavery has already been abolished. However, Huck, who by now has formed a deep friendship with Jim, has extreme pangs of conscience because he is about to help a slave gain freedom. Although he is himself anything but a respectable citizen, he still regards it as nothing less than a sin to do such a thing.[4]

In both these episodes, truly serious situations are involved, and moral questions are at stake. From them it can be seen that the ability to transgress prohibitions is one of the aptitudes constituting a moral life. As we know, Georges Bataille declared the transgression of prohibitions to be a sign of the sovereignty of a human being.[5] But that is not what is meant here – or at least, not quite what is meant. For what matters in a moral life is not the pleasure in freedom which Bataille associates with the transgression of prohibitions. In a moral life such transgressions can only occur in isolated cases, whereas the *ability* to transgress prohibitions is essential to a moral existence. To illustrate this by a relatively innocuous example: it is not especially moral to abstain from stealing *if one does not dare to do so*. And what is commonly meant by *not daring* does not need to be a fear of sanctions, but can simply be an inability to deviate from average social expectations, that is, from customary behaviour. The customary practice of not stealing can very well be adopted as part of a moral life – I am someone who does not steal – but to do so one must first have acquired the certainty that one *could* steal. It can be seen that to enter on a moral life does not everywhere and universally mean to violate customary behaviour, but that the transgression of certain prohibitions is necessary – for practice, as it were, or as a kind of paradigm – in order to embark on a moral life. On one hand, such paradigmatic transgressions enable one to adopt the prohibitions positively, and, on the other, they generate the confidence that, when *matters become serious*, one will be able to deviate from customary practice.

This act of 'making up leeway', as Heidegger called it,[6] cannot be achieved in a purely intellectual way. It is a practical act, and through it selfhood is founded. However, the moral life does not refer merely to aptitudes and single acts, but to a whole way of life. The retrospective appropriation will be more serious, and may not be achievable at all without some major biographical change of direction. Anyone who becomes aware of the possibility of a moral existence, whose eyes are opened, so to speak, finds themselves to be someone who, in a fundamental sense, has not previously been themselves at all. It seems to them that, biograph-ically, *everything just happened that way*. They were born in a certain parental home, attended a certain school, showed themselves to have certain gifts, and it then was customary for them to embark on this or that professional career; finally, they happened to meet and live with this or that person – everything just turned out that way. Now one cannot, of course, be 'the basis for oneself', as Heidegger puts it,[7] and, biographically, one appears to oneself as having in some way emerged from a mist. But, to achieve selfhood, it clearly is not enough simply to decide to be what one is, or has become, in any case; without a No, without a major turning-point in one's biography, selfhood cannot be attained.

Such biographical breaks are also associated with losses, and it is by no means guaranteed that after them one's life will be better. But, with regard to a moral life, it is in any case preferable to lead a life for which one is oneself to blame, than to spend it claiming that 'things just turned out like that'. There is, admittedly, a danger that – just because of the losses, and especially the loss of esteem in the eyes of others whom one has disappointed – one may experience the biographical break as itself something which just happened. It is all too easy to give up one's selfhood after a break or decision which has not turned out well; all too easily a bad conscience can lead one to be reclaimed by 'the others'. It can be seen that to lead a moral life and to be happy are not the same thing. More precisely, selfhood begins at the point where one can integrate negativity.

Negativity can even play an important part in a moral life, at least at the time of the turning-point. Simply by rejecting possi-bilities of happiness, whether they concern success, money or certain forms of recognition, one gains a consciousness of *being oneself*. For in a straightforwardly 'successful life'[8] one will never know whether one has not been merely pushed along, or has been favoured by fortune. One would not know whether this life was actually one's own. Now, I certainly do not wish to offer a primer in the 'pursuit of unhappiness',[9] but I do wish to help one to gain the courage to cope with unhappiness. A moral life does not need to be unhappy, but negativity is a part of it and gives it a certain contour. It is by the ability to integrate negativity into one's life that selfhood is decided.

As life in its positivity is always already in progress, the beginning of selfhood is a No, a resistance to the customary and a departure from what happens of its own accord. The ability to say 'No' is thus a basic virtue, or the initial skill called for by a moral life. But to say 'No' is not a single act performed once and for all; it can only be a paradigmatic act which sparks the awareness of being able to be oneself. The ability to say 'No' will be needed again and again in subsequent life, and each time it will bring with it special risks. I shall take as an example the possibility of saying 'No' to offers of therapy. The exposure to dependence on experts, precisely when matters become serious, is especially great in the medical field. The knowledge of the average citizen in matters of sickness and health today is minimal, or is made diffuse and confused by the reading of newspapers. The more one knows in this area 'as a lay person', the more unsure one feels. For this knowledge is alien to us, and merely refers us to the one who really knows, the doctor. The authority assumed by the latter is exerted systematically by the medical profession. It forms part of their professional expertise. But the lay person cannot see, and does not want to see, how flawed this knowledge is; they cannot assess the uncertainties of medical knowledge or the risks of treatment, nor do they want to. They are therefore handed over unconditionally to the treatments proposed by doctors. To say 'No' here, or even to resist by asking questions, by demanding explanations, costs a great deal. Above all, it means taking upon oneself the risk associated with the further course of the illness. The paradox is that one has to bear this risk in any case, but would rather pass on the responsibility to others, at the price of one's selfhood. For the ability to say 'No' is precisely what is at stake here, and with it the appropriation of one's own life. Moreover, it will be hard to stand by the choice if the decision turns out to be wrong.

We touch here on the problem of remorse. Just as one does not wish to take failure of the treatment upon oneself, one is also inclined to detach oneself from those decisions and acts which have been proved wrong by their consequences, or have met with opposition from others. This causes a split within selfhood. One cannot stand by one's own deeds, and becomes divided from oneself. There are people who think they recognize the morality of a person precisely in their remorse and bad conscience. But these are merely signs that the others have caught up with the one who has broken away, and have made him once more compliant to the customary and the expected. Remorse is not a sign of a moral life, but a symptom of its collapse. Anyone who is a self does not know remorse, since nothing happens to him which he has not wanted; he is the author of his acts. Of course, he can make mistakes, and actions can entail consequences which he has not foreseen. But that is not a reason to distance oneself from one's actions; rather, selfhood requires that one endure even guilt, and bear even the unintended consequences of one's actions. And anyone who acts must reckon with the fact that he will do wrong to others. They will call upon him to repent his actions. But, in the end, what use is that to them, or, conversely: what does one gain by forcing another to apologize? A small triumph, a humiliation, a denial of that person's self. Why not maintain respect and acknowledge that he had reasons for his actions?

Unhappiness and remorse are the snares which constantly threaten to drag one away from the path of selfhood. But if we have said that it is precisely the ability to integrate unhappiness into one's own life which constitutes a moral existence, then that also applies to mistakes. It is by the faults in the coat we wear that we recognize it as our own.

The ability to act

It is said that action is the true domain of ethics. Ethics is concerned with acting well. But what actually is action? And does everyone act? To act is distinguished from to let things happen, or to get something over and done with. If someone says he or she is *acting*, it has a strong sense, something is emphasized. Kant associated the concept of action with freedom. To act was to be the initiator of a causal chain; it connoted spontaneity. But does any such thing really exist? Normally, at any rate, we do not act. Life happens, and we get this or that done, meet expectations, fulfil requirements to perform. We are driven by our fears and hopes – perhaps, too, by our ambition and desire to count for something. But none of that can be called action.

Plato admirably clarified the relevant difference in his dialogue *Hippias Minor*. He states it in terms of *voluntariness* and *involuntariness*. Socrates's argument with the Sophist Hippias turns on the question as to who was the better man, Achilles or Odysseus. When Hippias tries to assert that Achilles was better because he was more truthful – whereas Odysseus was scheming and duplicitous – Socrates points out that on occasion Achilles, too, told lies. Hippias defends him by showing that the alleged lies were only utterances made under the influence of affect. But in saying this he fell into Socrates's trap. For Socrates now proves that the better man is the one who lies intentionally, since only he sees clearly the difference between truth and falsehood, and thereby controls it. Thus, in mathematics, the better calculator is the one who can deliberately make mistakes, whereas mistakes merely *happen* to the weaker one. In arguing this Socrates also expresses the ambivalence of voluntariness, and no doubt many of his listeners at that time, and many readers of Plato now, will side with Achilles and prefer the naive, well-intentioned man to the shrewd intriguer.[10] But one thing is clear: action implies voluntariness, and voluntariness is a state in which one is not just carried along, or in which something merely happens to one; it implies that one is at a certain distance to all that. This is not to say that the state of voluntariness actually defines the moral life; but it does make a start to that life, provides a precondition for it. And here, too, it must be said that this state does not come upon one willy-nilly; it needs to be tried out and practised.

What does it mean *to be able to act without being pushed along*? Does it mean, for example, to act without a motive – that is, from mere caprice? But what does caprice mean? It is clear that we are touching here on the problem of freedom, as it has been discussed again and again in ethics. In Kant, freedom is a kind of primordial causality, a non-empirical origin of action. That is only conceivable if, like Kant, one distinguishes between a *mundus intelligibilis* and a *mundus sensibilis*, and assumes that the subject of action belongs to the non-empirical world. But even Kant, who had this schema at his disposal, had to specify a motive for moral action, a 'mainspring' (*Triebfeder*) as he revealingly called it. He found it in respect for the law. But this takes him outside his transcendental theory of freedom and back into psychology. We, too, want to place the question about the ability to act on the empirical plane, though not in the sense that it implies observable behaviour – such proof would, strictly speaking, be morally irrelevant. The ability to act is empirical in the sense that it is a skill which can be practised.

The *ability to act authentically* should be understood as the possibility of doing something purely on the basis of reflection. This is the type of action which Socrates distinguished by the criterion of *voluntariness*. The question he put to the Sophist Protagoras in the dialogue of that name is characteristic in this respect: 'Do you hold knowledge to be a ruling element?' His question aims to establish whether reflection can become an agency guiding and initiating action. Protagoras counters this by citing the opinion of the many, based on their experience that they *are overcome by their desires*, or, expressed more generally, that their actions are motivated by something which drives or draws them on, by affects.[11] Accordingly, authentic action is said to be something initiated and guided in an affect-free, or at any rate an affect-independent, manner.

Now, I maintained in a previous chapter that the average working, transport-using member of technical civilization today is capable of precisely that type of action, that is to say, of cool, objectively appropriate behaviour. Admittedly, in this formulation the point at issue is somewhat weakened, since I refer to it as *behaviour*, not *action*. In the end, it is for self-examination to decide whether the kind of skill one has acquired in being able to control a technical device properly even when under affective stress, or in treating oneself as a thing when giving oneself an injection – whether this skill is sufficient to be regarded as a basic aptitude of moral life. I have already pointed out that the achievements of objectivity and affect-independent behaviour are not as a rule the outcome of self-mastery and moral decision, but of a kind of split. If that is indeed the case, then, for the sake of practice, one ought to seek out certain situations in which action based on reflection is sure to meet with affective resistance. I shall mention a few situations of this kind which are trivial in nature, but which by degrees become *serious*. To take one example, one should try walking calmly into a cold lake, without hesitating at any point. Of course, one *can* do it! One simply has to do it. The crucial point is that one does not have the self-awareness which is a prerequisite for moral action if one has not, at some point in one's life, had the experience that *one simply had to do something, and then actually did it*.

I shall mention another typical situation, which may be characteristic of the context in which these reflections on ethics first came into being and were presented in the form of lectures: the fear of examinations. Fear of examinations is a state of unfreedom in which one does not even have access to one's normal stock of knowledge. What is the nature of this fear, and how is it to be combated? It results partly from a feeling of dependence, of exposure, and partly from the pressure to produce a maximum of performance at a single given moment. It is entirely possible to master this situation if one has once deliberately removed oneself from it. My recommendation is that, for once, one should deliberately make mistakes. In this way one overcomes both the feeling of not being in control of the situation and the usual inner urge to achieve one's maximum performance. One recaptures the situation as one's own; from being driven by events one again becomes the author of one's actions. The paradox is that by once having decided to be worse than one could be, in the long run one is likely to be better than one would otherwise have been.

I shall mention a third situation. It has to do with overcoming embarrassment. The feeling of embarrassment is, of course, a feeling of dependence on the opinions of others. One fails to do a great many things in life, and, in particular, one fails to re-examine a great many things in life, because it would be embarrassing – for example, admitting a mistake, or phoning someone back, or going back because one has forgotten something. By this example of *overcoming embarrassment* one can see perhaps most clearly that the coolness which everyone is able to show today is not quite the same thing as moral aptitude. We have to do here with a kind of intra-ethical debate or struggle. Embarrassment is a form of shame, and shame – if I may put it thus – is an elementary ethical feeling. Practice in dealing with embarrassing situations is therefore, to an especially high degree, a preliminary exercise for a moral life. For what is at stake is the ability to break through customary behaviour when matters become serious.

Moral existence begins with the ability to act independently of demands (*Zumutungen*) and temptations (*Anmutungen*). In the traditional debate on freedom more attention has been given to temptations, in the form of drives and affects. Today, when the drives are muted in any case, it is demands which are more relevant. These are the average expectations which control behaviour. A basic principle of these expectations is that one should be like everyone else, that is, one should not be conspicuous. Against this background, one of the basic qualifications for moral behaviour is rightly referred to as 'civil courage'. This term denotes courage in civilian life as against courage in war. The remarkable thing is that this peacetime courage is often more difficult than courage in war. For in war – as traditionally understood – everyone charges together, whereas civil courage generally calls for behaviour which is difficult just because it deviates from that of everyone else. In former times civil courage had something of angry defiance about it, since it usually had to be shown not towards the majority but towards a superior, as *courage before princely thrones*. Today, the dominant authority one has to deal with is not, as a rule, an individual, but simply the majority. To assert oneself against it is especially difficult because one has oneself internalized that authority. One has rehearsed majority behaviour as one's own average behaviour.

In the history of the German Federal Republic there have been ample opportunities to practise civil courage. These were good

LIVERPOOL JOHN MOORES UNIVERSITY
LEARNING & INFORMATION SERVICES

occasions for practice because one was not on one's own, but could act jointly with others of like mind – even if against the majority and the organs of state. I am thinking of the anti-nuclear power movement, the opposition to the Frankfurt west runway, movements against the prohibition to practise one's profession, against the census, against rearmament, against nuclear waste transportation, and so on. These were undoubtedly acts of civil courage, since they often involved the overcoming of inner inhibitions, and because each individual had to decide for himself whether to take part, and, finally, had to take responsibility on his own. This resistance movement, which has been on the alert throughout almost the whole history of the Federal Republic, and is constantly revitalized by new controversies, has enabled millions of people in our country to practise civil courage and civil disobedience, and thereby to gain an awareness of the moral life. Just as at one time, when the nation was authoritarian and militaristic, it was possible to regard the army as the school of the nation, in the history of the Federal Republic it is the resistance movement which is to be considered as the school of the nation, since the Federal Republic is a democratic form of state. By occasionally and conditionally calling back sovereignty from the state, young people, in particular, have developed into conscious citizens. Through its wide repercussions, this form of *rehearsing a moral life* also became a contribution to the self-understanding of the society in which we live.

To mention one last example of the rehearsal of the ability to act, I would recall an idea I introduced as a joke in an earlier section – the idea that an official in a bureaucratic agency might get the idea of being brave. Against the background of the discussion of civil courage, this somewhat absurd example becomes more plausible. For civil courage involves the application in the civil sphere of a *virtue* which was actually developed in the military sphere, namely courage or bravery. In general, what is at stake in these examples is the possibility that moral ideas can be applied at all in the average civilized life – the life smoothed out by the imperative to perform, by conformity to the system, by security. The outcome of our presentation of technical civilization has been that, in the normal life of work and travel, morality is superfluous. That does not mean, however, that one should let matters rest there, that one should put up with this situation. Rather, it is worthwhile – just for the sake of practice – to take these everyday situations *seriously*. That is achieved, as a rule, by using the lever of traditional moral ideas, especially the classical virtues of bravery, magnanimity and honesty, or by seeing such everyday situations in terms of more universal principles, such as fundamental rights or human rights. By taking matters seriously on occasions, for example by demanding rights of participation or insisting on equality, by rejecting lies or deceptions imposed by expediency or by introducing a perspective of public welfare or the reproduction of nature into economic life, one will trigger the most amazing responses. The least vehement reaction of one's environment will be the accusation of *naivety*. This implies that anyone who adopts a moral standpoint is behaving in an ingenuous, childish manner and is still ignorant of the ways of the world. In particular, it will be pointed out that his ideas are unrealizable and without practical consequences. Further accusations in this connection are of utopianism and idealism. Both of these imply, again, that a moral life entails an unrealistic attitude to the world. Furthermore, the introduction of a moral standpoint is felt to be embarrassing, a *faux pas*. It can be seen here that the world of customary behaviour protects itself even on the meta-ethical level: it is customary to adhere to customary behaviour. But one will also have a quite different experience – earning applause, finding coalition partners and even, sporadically, realizing that things can actually be changed. The decisive thing, however, is that by occasionally taking everyday situations seriously one gains experience of what can happen when matters really do become serious. And in any case, our normal everyday life is itself a serious matter, in that it decides, in the long term, what kind of people we are and in what kind of society we live. And so it is worthwhile to take this life seriously from time to time.

Participation

With this idea of periodically taking seriously the kind of society we live in we have reached – perhaps too early – a central and, for the ethics being presented here, crucial point, namely the connection between moral existence and moral argumentation. By occasionally taking seriously, in our lived situation, the question of the kind of society we live in, we commit ourselves to that question in a way which is no longer purely argumentative. I have pointed out that the basic outlook of our society is a liberal one. This implies, in particular, the belief that the pursuit of individual interests has a beneficial effect on public welfare. It also means that while everyone has rights of participation, not everyone needs to exercise them, and that an individual's choice of a mode of life, including the nature of his private existence, his thoughts, feelings and religious conviction, is irrelevant to the structure of the whole. But it also means, conversely, that the social regulations which one considers necessary and which, on occasion, one may support by moral argumentation, need not have anything to do with one's own moral life.

I should like now to state as a core element of a moral life that one does not accept this dichotomy. It is practically a defining characteristic of *living within the customary* to make generous use of one's liberal rights without concerning oneself about protecting them or developing them further. It is a characteristic possibility of our form of society that the project of one's own life can be confined to the shaping of the private sphere, and that one's relationship to public life and politics can be restricted to paying taxes and occasionally voting. It is characteristic of our constitution that it defines the state in contradistinction to social life, and that the social existence of the individual is therefore possible without any political commitment. That this has not always been so, and must not necessarily be so, can be seen, for example, from the primal text on the theme of caring for oneself – Plato's dialogue *Alcibiades I*. In it the concern for oneself, the rehearsing of selfhood, the formation and development of the soul, which Socrates pro- poses to the young Alcibiades, is equated with his development as a politician, a *polites*, that is, a publicly effective citizen. For us, that equation is by no means self-evident; rather, becoming politicized, or politically committed, is a special sign of a moral existence. That is also seen, conversely, in the fact that, for us, *being a politician* can be a normal, modern professional activity – that is, it can be conformist, performance-oriented and respectable within the framework of the customary, and *without* any special political commitment.

In order to fill the moral life with content, it is necessary to establish a relationship between one's own project of a moral life and what is held to be right in argumentation and discourses aimed at establishing a social consensus. For the structure of a moral life which has been developed in this chapter up to now – under the headings of selfhood and the ability to act – has remained a formal possibility which has been characterized, in particular, by negative capabilities: distance, resistance, voluntari- ness. The problem contained in this was already formulated clearly by Socrates. To return once more to his thesis in the *Hippias Minor*:

if the better mathematician is the one who can deliberately make mistakes, and the better man is the one who does not say untruths by accident or under the influence of affect, but lies because he knows the truth and the difference between true and false – if that is so, why then does this better man do the good and not the bad? Socrates's lapidary answer to this problem is the thesis that 'No one voluntarily does the bad', because he naturally does not want to harm himself. This Socratic solution to the problem clearly rests on a basic trust in the moral world order – a trust we no longer share. We therefore have to look for another solution. This other solution consists in *taking seriously* our rights of participation, that is, understanding the possibilities of political commitment as those which *also* decide what kind of a human being one is. For by taking rights of participation seriously one relates oneself to concrete moral ideas, those which we have referred to generally as themes or *topoi* of moral discourse. This relationship can consist in attempting to realize these basic moral ideas in one's own life project. But – and this must be stressed – it can also be a negative relationship; that is, it can consist in a commitment to change these basic moral ideas themselves. Moral discourses, as we have noted, are not concerned merely with defining new social regulations on the basis of fixed themes, but also with problematizing these basic moral ideas in the light of new problems and new political and cultural developments, and with working towards the establishment of new basic ideas and customary practices. Here, the practising of alternative modes of life can go hand in hand with a political commitment which aims at changing what is socially customary, even to the point of changing fundamental rights or individual laws. In the history of the Federal Republic up to now this connection between moral and political commitment and alternative modes of life can actually be observed in many instances. It can therefore be said that the alternative solution – alternative in relation to a state of civilization in which one believed one could rely on the moral world order – consists in exerting oneself, through the project of one's own mode of life, on behalf of the moral world order. By *world order*, however, I refer only to the limited horizon of the basic moral consensus which constitutes our social conception of ourselves.

This politicization of one's own life-project is also necessary for another reason. I have emphasized at various points that the project of a moral life – in deviating from customary behaviour, for example, or in the idea of the patient who has 'come of age' – carries heavy risks. As a rule, one will be unable to bear these risks in isolation. That is to say that even if one wanted to bear them alone, one would nevertheless, through the consequences of one's actions, implicate the people close to one, family, friends and sometimes society in a wider sense. A characteristic example of this is a mode of life in which one does not seek by every means, i.e. from prenatal gene analysis to preventive abortion, to avoid disability. One can really only sustain such a life-project if one is supported in some way by one's immediate environment. It follows from this in principle that one cannot restrict the project of one's own moral existence to one's own person, but must extend it, through establishing a moral consensus with others – that is, through the formation of social groups – to encompass society as a whole.

By taking rights of participation seriously, however, one will relate concretely not only to the basic moral ideas of the society in which we live, but also to the state of civilization which constitutes the present conditions of being human, and to the historical background of the society in which we live. The project of being-human-well is accomplished against the foil of the universal conditions of life – that will be the subject of the next section. And when matters become serious our own conception of ourselves will not be a conception of human existence in general, but of a particular historical situation. Our own historical location is defined by our participation in a community of contemporaries. To take our own existence seriously, that is, to live it as a moral existence, means to relate oneself to the concrete here-and-now. Which problems one has to reckon with in one's own life, which possibilities one must prepare oneself for and in which political-historical context one must see present-day events – all this decisively influences the development of one's own moral skills. In this way one is necessarily related to the historical background which one shares with one's contemporaries.

Being-human-well

Ethics is concerned with the good. But what is the good? Plato and Aristotle defined it more precisely as the human good, *to anthropinon agathon*. We say that ethics is concerned with *being-human-well*. The use of the adverb implies that this formulation does not refer to an attribute of the human being, but to a quality of *being* human.

What is at issue, therefore, is not certain attributes which qualify one as good, attributes which were traditionally called virtues, but an accomplishment, the accomplishment of being human. This implies that one can be what one is in any case, namely a human being, in different ways, and in particular, more or less well. Here, too, the Greek conception that to be good means to be better can be discerned. Being-human-well sets one off from the mode of life of the many. It will emerge, however, that the attempt to be human well is not really a striving to achieve a goal, but rather an endeavour to engage fully in being human and to disown nothing which forms part of it. It has to do with the moderation which at the same time is a proud renunciation of anything over-exalted, which Camus advocates at the end of *The Rebel*: a moderation which has learned how to live and die and, in order to be human, refuses to be God.[12]

To engage fully with being human, to disown nothing which forms part of it, seems to be in contradiction to what we have sketched under the heading of the *moral life*. Were not precisely the ability to act and to resist characteristic of the moral life, and did we not thus follow the traditional concept of ethics, according to which will and freedom are the chief attributes of a moral life? To be sure – but the rehearsing of selfhood and the ability to act related only to the formal preconditions of a moral life, the content of which remains to be decided. A first step in this was taken in the section on participation. Here, too, we were concerned with commitment, that is, with taking seriously in one's own life the specific ideas one upholds as a participant in moral discourse. To be human well is not the antithesis of the project of a moral life; this project is its actual content. The reason why selfhood, detachment, resistance and the ability to act are prerequisites for being-human-well lies in the peculiarities of our state of civilization, in which we are continually denied the ability to be human, which is overlaid and concealed by technology and administration and repudiated by hybrid projects. Conversely, however, the possibility of saying 'No', of not putting up with what is given, of resistance, is an essential part of being human. It is just that, in our historical situation, this refusal to resign oneself is directed less against nature than against the second nature or, as Gottfried Benn formulated it, against the 'state-controlled extermination of all essence'.[13]

For this reason this section, unlike the previous one in which the moments of action and decision were predominant, will be concerned rather with nature – the nature we ourselves are – and with what it means to engage ourselves with the given, and to let something happen to us.

A human essence?

It might seem that, in order to discuss being-human-well, we need to know what it means to be human. Is there an essence of the human being, that can be fulfilled more or less well? If being-human-well were determined by such a human essence, then it would again become a project. One would have in view an ideal state of human being towards which one had to strive. It is true that, historically, humanity's conception of itself has almost always been formulated in terms of such ideals. Ideal human being was posited as reason, for example, or freedom, as a state to be reached, or realized through emancipation. Such definitions of essence as types of ideal human being are of great importance and have had a significant and dynamic influence on history through education and politics. And the desire for resistance and intensification inherent in them is undoubtedly an integral part of human existence. But in gazing towards those goals, humanity has overlooked and denied the human situation, which consists in seeking to transcend oneself towards ideals to which, for that very reason, one does *not* correspond. This starting-point from which one breaks away, the given being one finds oneself to be, *nature* – this, too, is a part of the human situation.

I shall elucidate this in relation to the traditional understanding of man as *animal rationale*, as a rational creature. According to the classical rules of definition which go back to Aristotle, a definition is formed by stating the *genus proximum*, the closest species to the one to which the entity to be defined belongs, and then the *differentia specifica*, by which it differs from the other species within that genus. In this case the closest species would be the living organism or animal, and the *differentia specifica*, the way in which man differs from all other organisms or animals, is identified as rationality. The actual essence, or *proprium*, of man thus lies in the *differentia specifica*. Man is man essentially through his rationality. It follows – and this is how the formula has been actually understood, and has been implemented through education in a comprehensive strategy – that man is the more human the more he develops his rationality and overcomes the animality within him. That is only one example. There are other formulae for ideal humanity through which humanity has historically evolved its conception of itself by projecting itself in terms of a certain ideal form, a whatness. Accordingly, to be a good human being means to correspond as far as possible to the determinants of this ideal. In contrast to that, we are concerned, in our attempt at *being-human-well*, to engage with the intermediate situation, the situation between nature and ideal, between facticity and project, and to subject ourselves in earnest to the implications of this situation. That does not mean denying the ideals, but it does generate an awareness of the losses and one-sidedness which are bound up with their pursuit, and of the price to be paid for its realization. And, in the late phase of modernity which we have characterized as technical civilization, it also compels us to come to terms with the given, to refuse to disown nature, and to be able to live with what we do not control. An average human existence in technical civilization is dominated by the ideal of security – an ideal which generates the illusion that illness has been abolished, which denies death, which estranges one from one's body and devalues corporeal existence. Since being-human-well is defined on the basis of the general conditions of the given historical situation – this is, in our case, of the state of civilization which has been described – being-human-well is concerned primarily today with the pathic, with letting something happen to us, with engaging with the given; it is concerned with integrating the nature which we ourselves are into our practical conception of ourselves.

Being nature

That we live within nature, that we are living creatures, organisms, has been made emphatically clear by the problems which, in the widest sense, are called environmental problems. The fact that we cannot *not* be of this world, that we are *in* the world, that we must live within the circulation of elements, has been made directly perceptible to us. That does not mean, however, that we have already overcome the conception of ourselves which is articulated, for example, by the formula of the *animal rationale*, or that we have integrated our natural being explicitly into this conception of ourselves. On the contrary, nature, which we ourselves really are, remains external to us, an object of natural science, an organism subject to certain reciprocal influences and which we manipulate by means of technology and scientific medicine. Under these conditions, it becomes a specific ability, a skill, not just to have nature in some way, but *to be nature*. 'Bodily existence as a task'[14] calls for a special kind of attentiveness, and has to be practised.

It must be stressed here once more that the decisive constituents of a moral life cannot be simply communicated in words, but have to be acquired through accomplishment and practice. A text can only point in certain directions and indicate a number of issues, fields or central agencies in relation to which the ability to 'be nature' can be developed. That we are nature is a fact. But the question is whether this fact remains external to us and merely happens to us. And being the nature we actually are will not be primarily a matter of intensifying our physical activities – in sport, for example – for by doing that we might simply make nature still more an object. Rather, it will be a matter of recognizing what happens to us as belonging to us. The first step, therefore, is to relativize our understanding of ourselves as 'I', or, as is sometimes said, to *expand* our consciousness. If, instead of this, I cling to the 'I' to which something happens, what happens to me remains external to me. Now, it would be absurd to say 'I' to this external thing, for, as long as I hold fast to my 'I', I could at most address this thing which happens to me as 'you'. Our relationship to our own bodies is an example of this. How difficult it is not merely to have this body but to be it, if one holds fast to the 'I'. There is no other way than, from time to time, to let go of this 'I' to some extent, or to engage in modes of being in which the 'I' disappears. The insights of psychoanalysis are undoubtedly helpful here, since they teach that the Ego is only an epiphenomenon, an agency mediating between the Id and reality, an agency acquired through painful socialization, and which can be put out of action in regressive states by fear, pain or sexual ecstasy, for example. Normally, however, the Ego is not merely a theoretical hypostatization but a fixed agency determining our everyday behaviour: I sit, I telephone, I make an appointment, I write a text. But – as *reflection* can still tell me – I cannot think if no thoughts come into my mind, I cannot act if the nature we ourselves are, the body, does not play its part, and I shall not wish for anything if nothing affects my emotions or no desire arises within me. *Practising* begins when one consciously accepts this dependence on our own nature. However, this will certainly involve a relinquishing of our own self, or a weakening of ego-consciousness, or an expansion of awareness.

Characteristic of such practising is the exercise of *letting ideas come into one's head*. This means letting go of the linguistic and logical controls which the 'I' normally exerts and which actually constitute the 'I', in favour of free association, openness, intuitive apprehension. The same applies to other areas, such as actions involving the body. It is well known that the 'I' is actually a hindrance to higher degrees of bodily performance. While alertness and consciousness are certainly highly important in gymnastics or dancing, they must not be ego-centred; what is required is a diffuse consciousness, an alertness of the body, and a very great confidence that what one *wants* to happen will happen by itself. It is the same in the realm of wishing and desiring. Strictly speaking, one cannot *want* to desire. This explains the great difficulty many people have in knowing what they actually want, or more precisely, what they wish or desire; it explains the practical dilemma in which we want something and yet that thing means nothing to us, is without any attraction. In order to wish for something, therefore, it is necessary to relinquish the 'I' to some extent and to give ourselves up to uncertainty with regard to what can appeal to us and can cause desire to rise up in us.

I have indicated some ways in which our dependence on our own nature, and therefore our concomitant dependence on what is not 'I', can be integrated into the performance of life. When one refers, in other contexts, to the fact that man is nature like any other organism, one has in mind the fact that human life takes place between birth and death, that humans must eat and drink, and are exposed to illnesses. Philosophical anthropology, precisely to the extent that it is ethically relevant, has always sought to integrate death into self-consciousness. The reason, no doubt, is that death has been seen as the greatest moral challenge. However, attitudes towards death have been highly contradictory. For some, a moral attitude to death lay in the attempt to overcome it, so that mortal life was seen as a means of working towards immortality, as in Greek thinkers, for example. For others, it was more important to live one's own mortality as such – as Christian thinkers have done, up to the philosopher Martin Heidegger. Admittedly, this thinking was often bound up with the Christian hope for redemption from death. It is noteworthy that the same attention has not been paid to the fact of man's being born – probably because being born is regarded, as a rule, as an act completed with birth. In fact, however, the state of having been born has at least as much importance for human beings as death. And from an ethical standpoint the state of having been born is not exhausted by the fact that at a certain time one has seen the light of day. Rather, it has to do with the fact that one has received oneself, as it were, as emerging from mist or darkness, and that this being-given-to-oneself can potentially extend throughout the whole of life. That this is so is shown, for example, by dreams, which constantly present us with new aspects of ourselves, and in which we can again and again appear as strange to ourselves. If, therefore, some philosophers, especially Kierkegaard and Heidegger, have called for life to be lived as 'life-unto-death', one might reply that it is just as important to conceive of one's life as an everlasting birth. I could imagine that some artists live in this way. What is generally at issue here is to attach less importance to the 'I', which is essentially an identity achieved through biography, in order to be able to surprise oneself, and, though seeing oneself as unfinished, to keep oneself open to possibilities of development.

The relationship to illness is of great importance for the moral life. Our technical civilization, especially in the context of technical-scientific medicine, inclines us to see illness as a disorder in relation to normality, and to suppose that such disorders can in principle be remedied. A glance at the statistics, or at our circle of closest acquaintances, is enough to convince us that this conception of illness is an illusion. Only a small minority of illnesses are *cured*; most illnesses are of the kind one has to live with, and, once out of childhood and early youth, there is practically no one who does not have to live with some illness or other. If one has once come to terms with this fact, it emerges as a basic ethical problem *how* one is to live with illnesses. This does not mean that one should define oneself, or even develop an awareness of oneself, as a sick person. Protesting against the illness, and sometimes rising above it by ignoring it, can be adequate responses. It would not be adequate, however, to deny the illness or to define oneself out of it, for being-human-well also means living one's own fragility and weakness, as well as one's having been born and having to die. Here, nature means what in the Christian tradition was called the creatureliness of the human being.

Being-a-part

It is ethical reflection on the human situation of being-nature that first gives rise to doubts as to whether being-human-well is possible *on one's own*. If being-human-well means really engaging with the human situation, and fully living what it is to be a human being, it soon becomes clear that the humanity of the human being cannot be fulfilled in isolation. The most striking example is sexuality. Because the human being, as an individual, only exists within the gender difference, whether this is understood as primarily a natural or a social difference, he or she can only fulfil the task of being-human-well by understanding himself or herself as a related entity within a relation, or a pole within a polarity, or, more generally, as a part of a larger whole. That does not need to mean that the *true* human life must be conceived as a process of fusion or identification with another person. That could amount to appropriation, and violate the respect one owes to others in their otherness, and the need to preserve their individuality. But one certainly can live in such a way that one produces a larger whole jointly with the other, and is engaged affectively by this greater whole. At any rate, practising the ability to be a part is essential to being-human-well. It implies openness and attentiveness towards that which one is or can be with another, and it also means exposing oneself to the other and being affected by what affects him or her. Practising such an understanding of oneself, and the corresponding behaviour, is not easy. But there are opportunities for it in playful situations in which team-behaviour is called for. Such abilities are required, above all, when a human group *without* hierarchization is to be created, as in modern partnerships and families. For whenever a group is organized hierarchically, the whole is represented by one individual, the head of the family, at the expense of degrading the other members.

The ability to be a part is especially crucial in one's relationship to one's children. Here, it is all too easy to regard one's child as a part of *oneself*. This means, implicitly, that one is oneself the whole. In this way, the child's rights are not acknowledged, justice is not done to his or her autonomy or to the fascinating emergence of a new spontaneity in the child. It is noteworthy, and also in some way frightening, that Emmanuel Lévinas – precisely the philosopher of otherness – fails to understand the relationship to the child. He writes:

> Filiality is still more mysterious: it is a relationship with the Other where the Other is radically other, and where nevertheless it is in some way me.[15]

Similarly, he states earlier in the same interview (p. 66) that 'the subject's ego is posited in its virility' and hence that 'the feminine is described as the *of itself other*'. It can be seen here how the metaphysical approach, with its insistence on the ego and identity, is unable to encompass being towards the other. The child does not experience itself as a part of its father or mother, but as a part of a 'We', and, in face of this, must laboriously bring into being its own 'I' by an effort of distancing. The parents, however, must, to an extent, abandon their fixation on their own 'I' in order to participate intuitively in the whole which they form with their child.

In sexuality, and in the parent–child relationship, one takes one's place in a complex which represents another important aspect of the being-nature of human beings, that is, the complex of generations. We have seen that even the Declaration of Human Rights postulates being born within and belonging to the 'family of man' as essential to being human. These two facts are not a programme for the individual human being, but are constitutive and given. By seeing oneself as a link in the chain of generations, and by consciously, through sexuality and the engendering of children, placing oneself within the sequence of generations, one accomplishes one's own being-human as a part of a larger whole. Karl Marx spoke in this context of the realization of our human 'species being'.[16]

Finally, I would mention solidarity once more as a possible mode of being-a-part. I defined solidarity, incidentally, when I spoke of 'letting oneself be affected by what affects the other'. If one is a part of a larger whole, such as a family or a relationship between two partners, and in a wider sense if one is a member of an association, this solidarity comes into being practically by itself. All the same, tendencies of distancing will always manifest themselves: What has that to do with me? Here, the important thing is to practise equanimity, and to live the reality of being-a-part which is inherent in the cases mentioned – the family or partner relationship. It is clear that this 'being affected by what affects the other' can have very far-reaching consequences. The illness of a child, completely changing one's daily routine or even calling for an entirely new life-plan, or a misfortune befalling an individual member of a small group, or, perhaps still worse, the guilt and failure of an individual member, can entail a major curtailment of life-prospects for an individual. It would be quite mistaken to define being-human-well at this point in terms of concepts such as responsibility, self-sacrifice or any such performance-related expressions. What is called for is nothing more than refusing to evade the issue, and being affected by what affects the other.

To the extent, however, that solidarity is defined as a form of the ability to be a part, this concept has not yet been revealed in its full scope. For we are still dealing here with the solidarity between people who belong together. In the case of solidarity as love of one's neighbour, that cannot, in general, be presupposed. We shall have to come back to this.

Temptations and demands

It is also a part of being-human-well to put oneself in the way of temptations and demands. This observation may be somewhat surprising, since in the last section selfhood and the capacity to act were characterized precisely in terms of independence from temptations and demands. The fact that human beings are exposed to these pressures makes up their natural and social being to an exceptional degree. They are, in this respect, vulnerable creatures, beings open to allurement and deception. To be sure, human beings are only themselves if they are able to assert themselves and to keep temptations and demands at a distance. But that is only a part of the truth. For anyone who is not touched by such pressures and does not have to meet social expectations has no cause to act. And anyone who developed selfhood and the ability to act solely on their own account would turn themselves into a kind of free-floating, extra-mundane being and in *that* way would forfeit their humanity.

I shall clarify this dialectic by an example. It is natural for a mother to be affected by compassion if her child falls ill. This is not just a case of caring for the child, but of being genuinely affected by what affects the other, of compassion. In going through what is happening to the child she is, in a sense, the best diagnostician – because she does not merely register the child's suffering from outside – and she is, in principle, best able to say what would benefit the child. Her being affected by the child's suffering also makes her highly motivated to act, and this energy undoubtedly surpasses anything that would be mustered by an impartial observer. However, if her concern and fellow feeling grow too strong, she is, in a sense, herself ill, and can at most be a communication partner and resonance-box for the child. To really help the child a certain distance and overview, and at least a degree of objectivity, are needed. That would save the mother from excessive haste and panic, and, above all, would enable her to consider alternative therapeutic measures.

We can see from this example that while being emotionally

affected is certainly a prerequisite for action, action also requires us to free ourselves from this emotion in a certain way. True humanity, or, better, the accomplishment of being-human-well, lies midway between, or rather in a constant transition between, the two possibilities. The two conceivable poles of behaviour, on one side over-identification and on the other cool detachment, are both thoroughly *human* possibilities. But being-human-*well* consists in the movement between them. I say *movement* advisedly because there is, strictly, no intermediate state, no midway position between emotional involvement and detachment, but only a movement between the two, a repeated crossing over by which one constantly engages emotionally with an event and then, in order to be able to act, detaches oneself from it.

Under the conditions of our advanced technical civilization it can no longer be taken for granted that one is emotionally affected by temptations and demands. There are various reasons for this. One has already been mentioned – the habituated coolness of behaviour and the displacement of emotional involvement to the realm of the fictive. Added to this is what – unhappily – is called the stimulus-overload coming from the media; in our context it would be better to speak of the over-supply and the contextless presentation of information and images which in other circumstances would be capable of claiming our human involvement. It is no wonder that a habitual blockade is set up against these solicitations. Finally, one should mention the rational organization of life itself, which seeks, in the name of the central value of safety, to make the individual wary of any excitement. Insurance policies are the best-known mechanisms of this biographical levelling. In most cases, of course, insurance is merely the stage-prop of an illusion. Health insurance, for example, plays on the illusion that one can insure oneself against illness. In fact, of course, it is the case that health insurance increases the risk of illness, in that it contributes to thoughtless living and a reduced sense of responsibility towards one's health. In reality, therefore, health insurance does not insure one against sickness, but acts as a buffer against the event of illness; that is, by spreading the cost evenly over life it makes the event less striking and ensures that care is provided. Its effect, therefore, is that while illness is not prevented its biographical importance is reduced. As a further example I would mention legal protection insurance. It has in many respects a similar effect on biography to that of health insurance. But in this case the increase in risk and the reduction of personal responsibility take on proportions that must be described as immoral. Legal protection insurance positively invites the holder to act irresponsibly – the experts will take care of the consequences – and, in particular, such a policy, by its nature, renders superfluous any attempt to resolve the case in question by human communication: the most trivial dispute between neighbours is passed to a lawyer.

To sum up: the conditions of technical civilization – that is, the normal behaviour of the transport-using, working person, the role of the media in our access to the world, the rational strategies and the preponderance of experts – buffer the susceptibility of the present-day human being, or even put him out of reach of temptations and societal demands. The tedium and monotony of the average life are then compensated for affectively by living in fictive worlds.

Under these conditions, to be human well calls for an explicit art of exposing oneself to and engaging with temptations and demands. Here, more than at almost any other point, it becomes clear that the central theme of ethics today is not, or not only, action, but the development of pathic capabilities, of an art of becoming involved. To be affected, to be exposed to experience, no longer happens by itself. Here, too, practice is needed.

If I speak of practice, it is not only because certain skills are required simply in order to be emotionally affected today, to be carried along, to open oneself, to empathize, but also because any involvement *must be selective*. Strictly speaking, in this area practice can no longer be clearly distinguished from the situation when matters become serious. If one allows oneself to be affected by something, even if just for the sake of practice, that is already a serious matter. It raises the question of how one is to behave. And it is clear that one cannot allow oneself to be affected by *everything*, and that to open oneself totally would not be to be human well. No more, however, could one describe the present-day ataraxy, the imperviousness to affect and the state of being 'gloriously aloof', as being-human-well. One can only humanly survive the 'overload' of news and images on the wretchedness of the world if one allows oneself to be affected by at least *something*, and involves oneself at least somewhere. It cannot be denied that a part of being-human-well is to allow oneself to be affected by emotional temptations and demands.

True (human) being. Dignity

The declarations of human rights and the German Basic Law attribute dignity to human beings as a part of their substance. But the safeguarded goods and the demand for social human rights show that there are preconditions for human dignity, and that it can be threatened. Moreover, as a theme of moral life, dignity is something which must have its reality, for each individual, in the *way in which life is lived*. One speaks, for example, of the importance of 'growing old with dignity'. Similarly, there are even institutionalized efforts to make it possible to 'die with dignity'. Eye-witness accounts of resistance in the concentrations camps indicate that, for those involved, what mattered above all was to *preserve the human face* – even if that meant committing suicide.[17]

These brief examples show very clearly the sense in which dignity is a characteristic of being-human-well. Human dignity consists, precisely, in enduring the relationship between involvement and detachment, facticity and project, in refusing to deny the tension between them but, on the contrary, explicitly living that tension. Thus, to grow old with dignity means to accept ageing and one's own nature, and the facts bound up with the frailty of the body. On the other hand, however, it does *not* mean simply abandoning oneself to this process, 'letting oneself go', as it is called. *Preserving the human face* means not denying one's frailty and dependence, but it also means not *shamelessly* capitulating to them.

One might also call this self-respect, although it might be better to speak of a *willingness to have a biography*. For that, no doubt, is what was traditionally meant by a biography: the collecting of the events and experiences of life to form a history of the self, *one's own* history. The conditions of technical civilization no longer permit a biography in the average case.[18] The reason is not only the flattening-out of biographical events already discussed, but also the fact that the average transport-using, working life is divided into sectors and no longer seeks to attain unity. To be human well means not accepting this situation, taking on oneself the effort of biography. To do this it is necessary to expose oneself to events but, on the other hand, not to lose oneself in them; it means preserving or, better, creating the unity of the person, through detachment and resistance, throughout the various circumstances of life, the different historical periods, and the functional and utilitarian relationships in which one is involved.

Through the 'will to biography' one does justice to the temporality of human existence. That which makes up the human is 'by itself dispersed'.[19] One can never at any single moment be wholly a human being; what makes up being human is possible only in succession, in *life*. But just because of this diffuseness we are constantly in danger of forfeiting our humanity. The will to biography is therefore the will to preserve, or to create, the wholeness of the human being. But the temporality of human existence is not only of importance when life as a whole is at stake, but equally in the *small* events of life. Human beings are creatures of a single day, said the Greeks, *ephemeroi*, that is, they are at the mercy of the day or, as Bertolt Brecht expresses it: 'we are only tenants, provisional ones'. This trickling-away of time happens in fact, but we usually notice it only in retrospect. In face of this, to be human well would mean to enter into ephemeral existence itself, to *lead* one's life in the act of living, and to feel its transience. Under the given conditions, that is possible, as a rule, only as an exercise, or, better, as a feast. For normally, i.e. as working, transport-using people, we are orientated towards goals, and what we do is unimportant as an act, compared to its result in terms of performance or value; or, in the case of transport, the journey and the time it lasts are of no consequence; what matters is the goal, and reaching it quickly. This destruction of life by function and result can only be countered by, occasionally, living ritually – that is, restoring the attentiveness, articulation and, above all, the time which are appropriate to the act of living itself. This will succeed best in festive contexts, or, conversely, if it succeeds, life will become a festival. In this way playfulness becomes a theme of ethics. But, at the same time, matters become serious. For on the question of whether one can lead this transient life serenely, or even, on occasion, festively, also depends *what kind of human being one is*.

Play and Seriousness

Play as an anthropological category

Play is an anthropological category – but to point that out is not enough. I would like to show that a closer consideration, in which *play* is set in relation to its counter-concept, *seriousness*, leads us into the field of morality.

It was the cultural historian Johan Huizinga who identified play as a central human attribute in his book *Homo Ludens. A Study of the Play Element in Culture.*[20] He does not deny that animals also play; on the contrary, he regards this fact as important. But the human being *goes on* playing, prolongs the game, puts it on a permanent basis, and from this arises what distinguishes human beings as human: culture. That is Huizinga's version of the thesis that the humanity of human beings consists in turning a weakness of their nature into a strength – the theory of humans as defective creatures (Protagoras), of the human being as the animal whose nature has not yet been fixed (Nietzsche), of the human being, as a physiologically premature birth (Gehlen). Animals, too, play, while they are growing up: they rehearse, imitate, try out experimental actions. In man, this adolescent behaviour becomes an institution of social life as a whole. Let us call to mind the three main characteristics of play according to Huizinga. The first is freedom: by freedom as the freedom of play Huizinga does not mean freedom in the strong sense which is usually reserved for human beings, but freedom from function and purpose: if someone plays, they do not do it for a particular reason – they *just play.* 'Child and animal play because they enjoy playing, and therein precisely lies their freedom.'[21] The second characteristic Huizinga refers to is predicated on the difference between play and seriousness: 'play is not "ordinary" or "real" life'.[22] Play is a piece of life which is placed, as it were, in brackets, takes place within a hypothetical, fictive space, is 'relieved of the burden of action', as one might say today. The third characteristic mentioned by Huizinga is the 'closed and circumscribed' nature of play. 'It is "played out" within certain limits of time and place. It contains its own course and meaning.'[23]

These characteristics have been selected, of course, to encompass both animal play and play within culture. If one were to adopt them as such, one might doubt whether culture as a whole could be seen as play, or a derivative of play. For is not human cultural behaviour purpose-directed, is it not thoroughly serious and, as culture, all-embracing? But that is not what is meant by Huizinga. By approaching culture through play, he throws light on the former. As freely structured, conventional behaviour, culture is a means by which humanity rises above the necessities of life and, within a circumscribed space of ritual enactment, discovers the meaning of life in life itself. In taking this view Huizinga harks back to earlier theories of culture, especially of the seventeenth and eighteenth centuries, according to which life, and particularly social life, is a game, a play on the great stage of the world, and the world is an imaginary space in which everyone acts their part, in which nothing is ever serious and no one is ever really themself.

Among these theoreticians of culture, Huizinga is especially close to the viewpoint of Schiller. In his letters *On the Aesthetic Education of Man*,[24] Schiller elevated play to a central anthropological category; for him, the metaphor of life as play was not a critique of *vanitas*, a comment on the illusoriness and irrelevance of social life, but a formula for an ideal, or, better, for a future, reconciled state of human existence. Against Kant, who located human freedom in reason and understood it as freedom from the senses, he posited it as freedom from the purposes of reason, and found the reconciled middle between these two concepts in play.

> The sense impulse excludes from its subject all spontaneity and freedom, the form impulse excludes all dependence, all passivity. But exclusion of freedom is physical, whilst exclusion of passivity is moral, necessity. Both impulses therefore compel the mind, the former through laws of nature, the latter through laws of Reason. So the play impulse, in which both combine to function, will compel the mind at once morally and physically: it will therefore, since it annuls all mere chance, annul all compulsion also, and set man free both physically and morally. (Letter 14)

No doubt, the dialectic in this quotation is somewhat too compressed. Schiller's idea becomes transparent through its relationship to Kant's *Critique of Judgement*. In it Kant had identified the free play of the mental powers, that is, of the senses and reason, as the basis of aesthetic pleasure. An object is described as beautiful by Kant if it gives rise to this free play of the mental powers. With Kant, but going beyond Kantian thought, Schiller saw in this free play true humanity, that is, freedom both from physical coercion and from the compulsions of morality. The idea of the sovereign human being makes its appearance here, a human being who can playfully engage in sensuality but also preserves autonomy in his or her moral life in face of the universal law. Even Kant had recognized, in the *empirical interest* in beauty (*Critique of Judgement*, §41), a need to share one's feelings with others, and therefore a force conducive to sociability.

Schiller hoped that through play human beings might escape the state of being torn between sensuality and reason, and might be liberated to enjoy the unity of their being. To the objection that this would 'strip reality of its seriousness',[25] he replies: 'But why call it a *mere* game, when we consider that in every condition it is precisely play, and play alone, that makes man complete and displays at once his twofold nature?' (Letter 15). True humanity only begins beyond necessity and beyond reality, and thus beyond seriousness: 'Man plays only when he is in the full sense of the word a man, and he is only wholly man when he is playing' (Letter 15).

The transition to ethics

Through the special status granted to it in both cultural philosophy and anthropology, play has a tendency to pass over into ethics. For if, like Huizinga, one sees in the continuation of play as culture that which distinguishes man from animals, or, like Schiller, elevates play into the mode of living of true humanity, in both cases a principle of difference is introduced, on one side of which is the good – that is, the good life as play. But the transition to ethics opened up by this introduction of difference also brings the opposite of play into view. Play is seen in contradistinction to ordinary life, to real life, to necessity, to seriousness. At the moment when one seeks to give play an ethical status by contrasting it to what is other, it suddenly appears in a different light. Elevated to a mode of life, it becomes the illusory utopia of an exceptional state made permanent, an unrealistic, fictitious attitude to life, an evasion of life's seriousness. It thus becomes *merely* an aesthetic mode of living, which is opposed to the ethical. That is how it was seen by Søren Kierkegaard. In his book *Either/Or*[26] he opposes the ethical mode of living, as that of seriousness and resolution, to the aesthetic mode, which is characterized by indifference and a refusal of *choice*. Precisely in face of the playful, free-floating, indifferent mode of life, seriousness becomes the decisive ethical category.

What is seriousness? In his book *The Concept of Dread* Kierkegaard tries to answer this question, in a section where he discusses 'certitude and inwardness'.[27] The answer is difficult to articulate since *seriousness*, as Kierkegaard observes, cannot be defined. But this observation *is*, in a way, the answer, since it leads to the discovery of a new type of concept, which Kierkegaard calls the existential concept. What Kierkegaard is concerned with is not 'serious' as an adjective, as the term is used when one says: 'he has a serious expression'. Rather, he is concerned with uses of the word 'serious' which occur in statements like: 'I am speaking seriously', or 'I take philosophy seriously', or 'Now it's becoming serious'. In these usages the word 'serious' does not refer to a property of something, but to the 'How' of an act of living or a mode of being or, to speak with Kierkegaard, the 'How' of *existence*. I can do philosophy just to pass time, for fun, or I can take it seriously. One can argue and fight with someone – playfully – and suddenly the situation can turn serious. I can say something just to contribute to the conversation, out of pure politeness, or I can speak seriously. Each time matters become serious what is at stake is involvement, when suddenly I myself am at stake and the affair in question is no longer just an affair but *my affair*. It is I who am affected by the particular content. For this reason Kierkegaard frequently speaks of subjectivity. The philosopher Hermann Schmitz refers today to the subjective situation: the unity of an issue and the feeling that it is *my* issue; in this self-consciousness lies the seriousness of the matter.[28]

The definition of a moral question

My thesis, now, is that what constitutes a moral question is determined essentially by reference to the concept of seriousness. A moral question is one through which *matters become serious*. Accordingly, there are two main types of moral question, depending on whether matters become serious for the individual or for society. For this reason there are two parts of ethics which are structurally different, although connected. Questions which are serious for me are those which decide what kind of a human being I am. They are answered by the projecting of a mode of life in practice. Questions which are serious for society are those which decide in what kind of society we live. They are answered by discourses concerned with conventions for regulating social life.

It is now time to justify this conception of ethics. It is usual to regard moral questions as those which are concerned with good and evil, or – to put it more professionally – those in which claims about the validity or correctness of maxims, decisions or actions are at issue. The term 'moral questions' is also used to refer to *questions of evaluation* or *questions relating to views of the world*. In all these uses of the formulation 'moral questions' it is assumed that the matter in question should be judged on the basis of other propositions. It is of little account that, as a rule, these other propositions have the character of values, norms or imperatives. What matters is that, according to this ordinary conception, moral questions are those which can be decided *hypothetically*. To give one example: in the well-known dilemmas used by Kohlberg and Piaget in investigating the development of moral judgement, it is regarded as a moral question whether someone who has no money is entitled to break into a pharmacy in order to save a dangerously sick relative. The moral aspect of such a question lies in the fact that it is to be decided on the basis of certain presupposed values or moral principles. That means, however, that the question is decided without anyone being affected by it, and, in particular, without the *person judging the question* being affected by it.

This ought to make clear why I propose a different conception of what constitutes a moral question, and have linked the meaning of moral questions to the existential concept of seriousness. The aim is to drag ethics out of the ivory tower of ontological, analytical and meta-ethical discourse and place it radically within reality. A moral question is *someone's question* in the radical sense that someone not only poses and weighs the question, but, through it, ·calls himself into question. And a moral question is one which a society poses to itself, not in the sense that it is debated in public or philosophical discourses, but in that it decides the kind of society in which we live. Admittedly, moral questions are indeed decided within the horizon of general value-conceptions, whether of a material or formal kind – such as the value of life, the value of property or the principle of democracy and living together under the law. However, it is not that which makes them moral questions, but the fact that, through them, matters become serious, whether for me or for the society in which we live.

The first justification of this conception of what constitutes a moral question, and consequently of ethics itself, is derived from Kierkegaard's analysis of seriousness. The fact that a question is serious for me means that at the same time this question concerns me. The matter or circumstance addressed in the question is one which affects me, is one in which I am involved in such a way that the decision of the question regarding this circumstance also decides how and what I am. What is at issue, therefore, is a *subjective situation* the problems of which can never be solved hypothetically but only by existence.

This justification of the conception of a moral question as one through which matters become serious applies first of all, of course, only to the part of ethics concerned with the moral existence of the individual. Its application to the social sphere and to the moral meaning of questions debated in public discourse is only an analogy. For, strictly speaking, a subjectivity cannot be ascribed to society as a whole, since we who describe it can never be society itself. Moreover, we do not consider our society from outside, but only as *participants* in public discourse. If, in public discourse, one defines moral questions as those through which matters become serious, that means that our common understanding of the kind of a society we live in – for example, whether it is a liberal society, a democracy, a peace-loving society, a society with solidarity, etc. – depends on these questions.

To sum up, therefore, we can say with Kierkegaard that moral questions are those through which matters become serious because they are *existential* questions.

Are moral questions uncommon?

Moral questions are uncommon. With this thesis we come back to the relationship of seriousness to play. For just as play is defined on the basis of seriousness, so is seriousness on the basis of play. That moral questions are rare means that ordinary life is not, as a rule, serious: that is, it is a game, or practically a game. That does not prevent people from ordinarily taking it dreadfully seriously, and carrying on as if it were serious. But before expressing such criticism it is necessary to state why, in what sense, ordinary life is not serious. What does that mean, and why is it the case? The first and most important reason is the conventional way in which daily life runs its course. One follows the conventions because they are conventions – but they might also be different. One stays within the bounds of the customary, and as a result the question as to who one is oneself does not arise. The second reason is the general replaceability of everyone. Ordinary life is so organized that, wherever it is possible at all, I could be replaced by someone else with similar competence. The average life of work and mobility neither requires me as myself, nor does its functioning depend specially on me. On the contrary, it functions all the better the less of my subjectivity I bring into it, that is, the less it has to do with me and the more I myself merely correspond to general functions in which I am in principle replaceable. In sociology that is called role-based behaviour. The human being is integrated socially by means of specific roles he plays. In the end, what matters to society as a whole remains, as a rule, external to the individual. There are fashions and trends, political tendencies, rivalries and ideologies. All of this could be different, and the individual simply plays the game. That even applies to questions which have serious implications for society. The structural difference between the moral questions which affect the individual and the moral questions which affect the conventions for regulating social behaviour is precisely what makes it possible for the individual to participate fully in public and moral discourses without it thereby being decided what kind of a human being he is. A German doctor, for example, can reject euthanasia on the basis of general considerations, such as the lessons of historical experience, and yet facilitate death in an individual case in which he is personally challenged. It can be seen here, from the perspective of seriousness, how the Kantian categorical imperative is seeking to yoke together by force two parts of ethics which do not necessarily belong together. The reasons why one can want something to become a general law have to do with our social conception of ourselves, but not necessarily with how well one is human or with what kind of a human being one is.[29] I said 'not necessarily' – in an individual case, of course, it may happen that someone makes a public concern their own. But in general, politics and public discourse are *not* a serious matter for the individual.

To recognize this and, more generally, to recognize that ordinary life is *not* serious is, paradoxically, the beginning of morality. I said just now that people frequently take ordinary life dreadfully seriously and behave as if it *were* serious. That does not mean, however, that they are not aware of the conventionality of their behaviour. They take conformity to customary behaviour to be morality, they nourish their self-confidence on the illusion that they are irreplaceable, and they believe that they are realizing themselves when they are merely following fashions and trends. To see through life as a game and to take part in it as a player, competently but calmly, actually places one in a position where matters can suddenly become serious. On this point Schiller was right: life as play is indeed the state of freedom – that is, the state in which one can distance oneself from what goes on, what is customary, and confront life with serenity. But this state is, after all, only the beginning and the precondition of morality. Thus, Kierkegaard defines the aesthetic mode of life, the mode in which one stands playfully outside life and enacts one's life as a game, as a preliminary stage on the path of life, on the way to the ethical mode. This transition takes place at the point where matters become serious.

From this we derive the second reason for defining what a moral question is through its relation to seriousness. Seriousness is that which breaks through the arbitrariness of life. Matters become serious when customary practices no longer count, when we become irreplaceable and when the goals we pursue in ordinary life are no longer merely external to us.

Moral questions are those through which matters become serious because they present themselves bindingly.

When do matters become serious?

It is this binding nature of seriousness, we can say now, which breaks through ordinary life – the life in which one is always replaceable and everything could always be different. When matters become serious we are challenged as ourselves; we cannot evade the challenge, and must respond existentially. These, then, are the two characterizations of seriousness. A question, a situation is serious when it challenges us bindingly and when we must respond by the way we live our life. But when do questions and situations become serious?

In the analogous case, when a question or a problem is serious for society's conception of itself, it is easy to give an answer: when the basic moral ideas which determine society's conception of itself are touched upon or challenged.

The question as to when matters become serious for someone cannot be answered in general terms because what is at stake at that moment is, precisely, the kind of person he will become. But what one can say is that seriousness breaks in at times of decisive or critical biographical constellations. That is, as such, a tautology, since such constellations are the very ones in which it is decided what kind of a human being the person in question is. But it does lead on to the ethical doctrine of the *kairos*, of the right and decisive moment. Since antiquity this doctrine has raised the question of the temporal nature of moral action. For it states that, from a moral standpoint, there are differences between times. For most of the time life runs its course as if by itself, or is carried along by customary behaviour. But there are constellations which interrupt this continuity, and on them depends what kind of a human being one is and how one is to continue in normal, customary life. The doctrine of the *kairos* also contains two further moments: on the one hand, it states that the *kairos* is a constellation, that is, a situation which does not depend solely on the person concerned, or on that person's immanent development: the *kairos* is something which befalls the individual concerned. On the other hand, the doctrine of the *kairos* points to the importance of alertness or, better, readiness. The doctrine states that one can miss one's *kairos*. Consequently, the project of a moral life calls for attentiveness, a flair for the decisive situation, and a readiness to be resolute when the situation arrives – that is, not to ponder endlessly and postpone decisions.

However, that does not say enough on the question as to when matters become serious. For the *kairos* could also be a favourable opportunity for something one always intended to do in any case. We do not wish to understand it in that way here, but as the situation in which matters become serious. *What* makes them become serious?

This question, too, cannot be answered in general terms since it always poses itself for the individual in a particular situation. One can, however, identify what makes a certain situation or constellation serious for an individual: namely, the fact that they are challenged as the human being they are. Something of this kind must be contained in the situation which hurls in the individual's face the message: *tua res agitur* – now it is for you to act. For only in this sense are they struck, affected. There must be in the situation, accordingly, something which addresses or appeals to the individual concerned, and makes them aware both that the situation is inescapable and that they are an irreplaceable part of it – *Hic Rhodus, hic salta!* Now it's serious, you can't make any more excuses: now show who you are!

Naturally, this should not be understood to mean that the individual concerned could not find excuses or evade the issue. For the fact that one can miss the *kairos* is one of its characteristics. Thus, while it can be said that the seriousness stems from the constellation, one must, as the person concerned, engage with it. But that there is a certain preponderance of the constellation over the individual, that the seriousness really comes upon them, can be seen from the fact that even evading the issue has consequences for the kind of human being they are.

That the seriousness which makes a situation into a moral challenge stems from the constellation has been described in different ways in the recent debate on ethics. I should like to mention two instances, Emmanuel Lévinas's conversation of the 'face' and Hans Jonas's discourse on responsibility.

In his reflections on the human face Lévinas attempts to show that the other human being, purely through his or her manner of appearance, contains an appeal that we be affected morally. By the term 'face' he refers primarily to the human face, from which, no doubt, this appeal does emanate. But, on the one hand, he does not want necessarily to restrict himself to the face, but refers to the whole appearance of the human being, and, on the other, by the term 'countenance' he would like to articulate the vivid or holy quality of this appearance, in other words, its moral appeal. This appeal, for Lévinas, has primarily the character of a prohibition. The face says: Thou shalt not kill. By interpreting it in this way he derives from the appeal, or attributes to it, an ambivalent character. For where there is a prohibition there is also a challenge to transgress it. In the manner of experiencing the countenance Lévinas also sees an invitation to murder. Understood more generally, though in a weaker sense, the 'manner of encountering the face' is an experience of the other who *appeals* to me, or, to put it more aptly, of *my* other. We can then say retrospectively with Schmitz that the other is part of my subjective situation, or that the other demands that I respond with seriousness. The primary response to this demand, according to Lévinas, is language.

This brings us very close to what Jonas understands by *responsibility*. For Jonas, responsibility is the response to a moral demand emanating from a situation, whether it arises from a person or a thing. In his discussion of this demand Jonas does not remain on the phenomenological level but attempts to justify its possibility ontologically. He finds this possibility in the observation that there are entities which have their ends within themselves. This has been defined most clearly by Heidegger in his *analysis of Dasein*, that is, of the human being as an entity. Human beings are entities in whose existence their being is at stake. To perceive such being as endowed with an inner purpose means, according to Jonas, to be conscious of an appeal to serve this inner purpose. Of course, one must be receptive to such an appeal, or open oneself to it. One can also, however, close oneself and make the being with which one is concerned into a pure thing or fact. The prototype of a situation in which responsibility for a certain entity is called for is the parent–child situation. 'This is obvious for parental responsibility, which really, in time and in essence, is the archetype of all responsibility (and also, genetically, I believe, the origin of every disposition for it, certainly its elementary school). The child as a whole and in all its possibilities, not only in its immediate needs, is its object.'[30] To be together with a helpless child is, Jonas says,

LIVERPOOL JOHN MOORES UNIVERSITY
LEARNING & INFORMATION SERVICES

to experience the demand to help this being. He even believes that an origin of morality in natural history can be identified in this demand. Responsibility in Jonas's sense is the existential manner in which I react to such a demand. Its structure is therefore asymmetrical. I have a responsibility for someone, but that person has not necessarily a responsibility for me.

In the passage mentioned, Jonas discusses the parent–child relationship. Undoubtedly, however, he does not want what he says about the moral demand which emanates from an existent being, and the responsibility corresponding to it, to be limited to the preconditions of this situation. For in a parent–child relationship we must assume that the partners already belong together from the start, so that the care for the child might in some cases also be care for oneself in the narrower sense. The solidarity in which one allows oneself to be affected by what affects the child could also be founded in a prior 'We'. To make this point still clearer, I should like to recall the parable of the Good Samaritan from Luke 10: 25–37.

Jesus relates this parable in response to the question: 'Who is my neighbour?' This question arises compellingly from Christian ethics, the fundamental commandment of which is charity or love of one's neighbour. Does charity require, for example, that one should love family members, neighbours, members of one's club, fellow citizens? The answer Jesus gives through this parable is: my neighbour is the human being who needs me in a chance constellation – whoever he or she may be.

> A certain man went down from Jerusalem to Jericho, and fell among thieves, who stripped him of his raiment, and wounded him, and departed, leaving him half dead. And by chance there came down a certain priest that way: and when he saw him, he passed by on the other side. And likewise a Levite, when he was at the place, came and looked on him, and passed by on the other side. But a certain Samaritan, as he journeyed, came where he was: and when he saw him, he had compassion on him, and went to him, and bound up his wounds, pouring in oil and wine. (Luke 10: 30ff)[31]

By making the priest and the Levite fail to meet the moral demand represented by the injured man, Jesus undoubtedly is directing his barbs against the professional good people of his society. What is more important, however, is that he refers to the man who helps as a foreigner, who therefore has no original relationship of solidarity with the injured man. In his action the Samaritan merely responds to the moral appeal which is presented by the wounded man's need for help.

With regard to our question as to when matters become serious, what we can learn from the parable is that the situations in which matters become serious certainly do not need to be prepared for in our own biography, but can be constellations in which we find ourselves unawares. And the obligation they entail – this is the other point – certainly does not need to be determined by a pre-existing bond to the persons or things forming the constellation. On the other hand, one should not interpret the examples mentioned – the parent–child relationship, the Good Samaritan – in a restrictive sense in which the seriousness which makes the situation a moral one always emanates from persons, or even from persons who suffer. These examples have only been chosen because they are the most immediately plausible. But, naturally, situations of political struggle or of co-operation in work, or perhaps even relationships within or to nature, can also be of such a kind that one feels: now you are being challenged, now it is up to you. But equally, the examples should not be understood to mean that the seriousness of a situation can only come from outside. If one has chosen a moral life or wants to practise a moral mode of life to any degree, it is entirely possible to take a situation seriously which, in the daily life of work and travel, is not serious at all, that is, which could be dealt with within the framework of customary behaviour. That would mean not letting things just happen, but making them one's own concern. Even if it should be noted that seriousness is something which is primarily experienced passively, nevertheless this transition to an active mode of behaviour by which, through commitment to a cause (or to persons), one makes it or them one's own concern – this transition is crucial in giving lasting content to a moral life. That would probably also be an appropriate interpretation of the current discourse about self-realization. For self-realization cannot, as is popularly supposed, be founded on something pre-existing within the self, but consists in giving content to selfhood by taking seriously something outside oneself, that is, by making a situation determined by persons or things one's own concern.

This manner of taking seriously should not, however, be confused with the everyday way in which business, chatter or customary behaviour is taken seriously. It remains the case that seriousness only receives its determination in contradistinction to play. Seriousness characterizes the moral life precisely because it does not encompass the whole of life. The conception of life as play, and the distancing implied by it, remain preconditions of a moral life. Only someone who knows ordinary life to be a game and can play it will occasionally, and at the decisive moment, take situations seriously.

— 4 —

Moral Argumentation

Moral Questions Concerning External Nature

With this chapter we are entering the second part of ethics. Whereas the theme of the first part was the project of a moral life, the discussion will now turn to the moral arguments involved in establishing social conventions. Such conventions are either laws – in which case they are explicitly binding on every member of society and are sanctionable – or they involve customary behaviour. As in the case of laws, we have not included customary behaviour itself in philosophical ethics; but we have included the arguments in which it is problematized, or in which new customary practices are established. Practical debates are initiated if customary practices have been called into question, or if they prove no longer adequate to new developments, in which case there is a need for *regulation*. However, not every debate which is supposed to lead to the establishment of new laws or customary practices requires moral arguments. A question or a problem which is in need of regulation should only be considered a moral one if it touches either on our conception of ourselves as human beings or on our society's conception of itself. Many questions can be regulated in a purely pragmatic way. The standard example of such morality-free arrangements are road traffic regulations.

In what follows I shall discuss three examples – one in each section – of moral discourses which have led to new social regulations, or are pushing society towards them. The choice of such examples is somewhat difficult. An ethics is not itself a contribution to ongoing discourses, but nor should it merely report on them. In principle, it should make clear what such discourses involve, and prepare the reader to take part in them, or to take part more effectively. This means that one should be as concrete as possible, but this concreteness can have the result that what is said quite quickly goes out of date. I shall therefore choose problems on which the debate has been continuing for some time and has already found partial solutions by establishing new conventions, but which deal with matters of such intrinsic importance that further discussion can be expected. These questions concern, firstly, external nature, secondly, the nature that we ourselves are, and thirdly, problems concerning the way in which society deals with foreigners.

The need for regulation regarding external nature

Let us begin with terminology: in using the term *external nature* I am following customary linguistic usage, although it can be expected that impending new social conventions concerning nature will change this form of conceptualization. For it will emerge that what is to be progressively overcome is the idea that *the nature which we ourselves are not* is external to us. In the case of what earlier was called internal nature the terminology has already been changed, so that I speak of 'the nature which we ourselves are'. For in this case it is clear that one is not talking about something internal, but about the body.

That there is a need for regulation concerning external nature is so self-evident that it requires no further demonstration. The problems which give rise to this need for regulation are generally called environmental problems. They concern the destruction of the environment in the sense of the disturbance or abolition of natural cycles, and the dissipation of substances and energy, especially poisonous substances such as heavy metals, or those which make the soil infertile, such as salts. They also concern the use and scarcity of resources and, finally, the fact that, in industrial society, external nature, in its parts and in its essence, is being turned into components of industrial machinery, and that, in scientific society, there is an increasing use of nature, and above all of test animals, in the acquisition of knowledge. These facts call for new social conventions for various reasons. The main reason is that through environmental destruction man is endangering the foundations of his own life, is poisoning the media and means of life and is generally increasing the risk of illness. In addition, however, the increasingly comprehensive nature of industrial production and the more and more radical and extensive encroachment of science on nature have made it clear that violence is being done to basic values of a kind which did not require explication, or even explicit formulation as fundamental values, earlier, i.e. a hundred or even fifty years ago.

The need for regulation which arises from these problems is already being met in numerous ways. Indeed, it can even be said that there is a surfeit of regulations – that is, of laws, decrees, resolutions, directives, standards, and so on. This is explained by the fact that up to now the necessary fundamental rethinking, especially with regard to the relation of man or society to nature, has not properly begun, so that attempts are made to find an individual solution for each individual problem. Moreover, the existing regulations have not been systematized. For example, given the plethora of laws relating to nature, it is necessary as a general principle to create a separate environmental statute book, comparable to the civil code or the penal code.

To illustrate the point, I shall list some of the problems. Nature protection probably has the longest tradition. In this context one should mention the preservation of the diversity of species and valuable ecotopes, and the protection of landscape. Many problems result from industrial production methods, and particularly from by-products and production residues, that is, industrial waste and emissions, and from the products themselves, such as CFC gases, which can have a nature-destroying effect. On the other hand, one must also consider consumer habits, or the economic organization of consumption, that is, methods of distribution and transportation, and above all packaging and waste. A particularly grave problem of industrial residues concerns radioactive waste from the so-called peaceful use of atomic energy. Finally, the problems concern resources, and their economical and rational use.

Another complex of problems is the relationship of people to animals. This relationship calls for regulations in the mass farming of animals, in the use of animals in science and, finally, with regard to the impending design of genetically modified animal and plant species.

As a last general problem, I should like to mention the treatment of nature as property. This problem has been discussed for a long time under the heading of *common land or private property*,[1] but is now gaining new topicality in connection with animal protection and the threatened patenting of genetically manipulated species.

This very unsystematic listing of the problems we have with nature, with its life forms and its parts – problems which call for social regulation – inclines one to ask whether all these regulatory questions are really *moral* problems. Are not many of them capable of being solved technically or purely pragmatically or, in a narrower sense, *conventionally*?

Why are these questions moral questions?

The ban on CFCs, for example, is not a moral question. Once it is known that CFCs act as a catalyst in a process which destroys the ozone layer in the upper atmosphere, it is clear that the production and use of these substances must be limited and, if necessary, prohibited. For the ozone layer acts as an absorber of dangerous ultraviolet radiation emitted by the sun, which can cause cancer in humans and animals and has a number of other harmful effects. This situation simply requires a practical solution. Given sufficient knowledge of the processes concerned, there are compelling reasons not to emit any further CFCs into the atmosphere. It is *more* of a moral question that agencies have kept quiet about this factual knowledge, which has existed for a long time, or have not paid attention to it. But on this issue neither our conception of what society is to be nor our self-understanding as human beings is at stake. What is fundamentally involved is the political question of enforceability in face of certain lobbies. Nor are most regulations concerning emissions levels – for example, in the context of emissions-control legislation – moral questions. Of course, morally dubious behaviour can be involved in disputes about threshold values for emissions, but in principle we are concerned here only with scientific knowledge and a process of political negotiation and enforcement.

The situation is different whenever nature is invoked in discourses on the introduction of new conventions. As we have seen, nature is a fundamental ethical value, or a *topos* in moral discourse. Nature is a value of the modern age, and one through which the self-criticism of modernity has been articulated. This is why it has taken on such importance at the present time, when the project of modernity is in crisis. Whenever one appeals to nature or naturalness in discourse, one is arguing morally, simply because nature is a moral value, and especially because our social understanding of ourselves and our conception of ourselves as human beings, in so far as both our society and we ourselves are *modern*, are called into question by the appeal to this *topos*.

I have already mentioned that it cannot be predicted in advance precisely what will form part of our fundamental moral conceptions. That they include nature is, of course, well known, but it is only the inclusion of this *topos* in discourses that will make fully clear what the moral evaluation of nature really entails. Initially – in the eighteenth century – the homage paid to nature was essentially aesthetic. Nature was recognized as beautiful and sublime, and was experienced as such through an entirely different mode of apprehension to that which had become dominant through natural science – that is, through a sensuous mode of experience. From this aesthetic admiration of nature there was – explicitly in Kant[2] – a transition to a moral evaluation. Nature was esteemed for generating order from within itself – something that human beings had to achieve by a moral effort. This role of nature as a moral example is to be found in Rousseau, in the concept of the natural state, and Rousseau's concept was itself derived from a tradition going back to ancient Greek Sophism. However, this moral valuation of nature was by no means a consensus; on the contrary, nature could be seen – as in Hobbes – as harsh and violent, so that the transition to civilization was justified as an overcoming of nature. The admiration of nature for its *technology*, that is, for the artistry it displayed, above all, in the inner functioning of organisms, was, however, universal in the eighteenth century. Against the background of this tradition, nature became a moral authority. But it had not yet become an object of moral behaviour or of moral demands. That only happened with Schopenhauer in the nineteenth century and with Albert Schweitzer in the twentieth. In his concept of reverence for life Schweitzer summarized, or heightened still further, the existing aesthetic valuation, moral respect and technical admiration for nature.[3] With his principle 'I am life that wants to live amid life that wants to live' he introduces a development in which nature is no longer only a moral *topos*, but in which the question of nature itself becomes a moral question. In what follows, this will be clarified in relation to two examples from recent history and the present. In the first example I shall discuss the new German animal protection law and, more generally, the question of our relationship to animals, as far as it calls for social regulation. It will prove to be an example of a moral question in that it impinges on our understanding of ourselves as human beings. The second example will concern a problem which is moral in that it affects our society's understanding of itself. This has become manifest in the adoption of nature as a good to be safeguarded in Article 20a of the German Basic Law. More generally, it will concern the question of a revision of our conception of production as appropriation of nature.

Questions affecting our conception of the human being

How can a need for regulation of the relationship between man and animal actually come into being? For we are not concerned here with a threatening situation caused by the specific behaviour of human beings, which can therefore be curtailed or ended – as in the case of the hole in the ozone layer. With regard to the tormenting of animals, it is not we humans who are damaged, but animals. The need for regulation through social debate does not arise directly from the damage, therefore, but from the anger it causes. This situation is somewhat paradoxical, in that something which primarily concerns non-human nature, that is, animals, becomes relevant to practical discourse through a human phenomenon, the indignation to which it gives rise. This situation suggests that animal protection is a genuinely moral question. In fact, it can be observed that in their indignation human beings take on a certain function of advocates for animals, of stewardship. The fundamental principle of the animal protection law will turn out to be a comprehensive formulation of this stewardship.

Indignation is only expressed, of course, when something in the relationship of human to animal has become intrusive, that is, has deviated from what was previously customary. And this indignation will only give rise to politically effective lobbies such as animal protection societies or associations for the prevention of animal experiments, etc., if the intrusive behaviour in relation to animals has fractured society, has split it into those who act and those who observe. For those who act it is, of course, their activity itself which is customary, as the customary practice of their industry, for example. It is of interest here to note what first triggered the formation of a public animal protection movement. It was the treatment of cab horses. The treatment of horses in agricultural service and in the military sphere was generally known and accepted. In addition, the horse had long enjoyed an especially respected position in Germany, probably connected to the comradely relationship which had existed between the knight and his horse. Because of the general respect for horses the eating of horse meat was frowned upon. Now, in the postal service there had undoubtedly been a ruthless exploitation of horses over a long period. But the people who observed it were travellers, so that they could always register it as an occasional case that had happened in a place they had already left. That changed when the horse-drawn cab became a ubiquitous means of transport in cities. Now the exploitation of horses was carried on before a public audience which, in addition, was actually in the role of observer – that is, it had nothing to do either with agriculture or with military service. It was this special constellation which first drew attention to the exploitation of horses and led to a split in society. This background was reflected in the first Animal Protection Law, §360, item 13 of the Penal Code of 1871, in which the tormenting and brutal mistreatment of animals were made a punishable offence if they were causing public outrage.[4]

Further causes of indignation resulted from the extensive use of animals as experimental objects in science, and from the advancing industrialization of agriculture. These two causes were primarily responsible for the German animal protection movement and animal protection legislation, up to and including the last amendment of 1998. The extensive use of animals in science – or perhaps one ought to say the misuse of animals in science – resulted, on the one hand, from the 'scientification' of medicine since the nineteenth century, and especially from the emergence of modern physiology, and, on the other, through progress in pharmacology. With regard to pharmacology it must be added that what is at stake is not just the development of effective chemo-pharmaceuticals, but, above all, their testing. The increasing stringency of approval regulations for new drugs necessitates more and more extensive tests for toxicity, side-effects, long-term consequences, and so on. The progress of experimental physiology and pharmacology contains the paradox that while these sciences are really concerned with knowledge of the human organism and the development and testing of drugs for the human body, animals are used in order to preserve this body. The attrition suffered by animals for the sake of research seems to cause less concern the more distantly the animals are related to man, but it can only yield relevant knowledge if the animals used are closely related to man.[5] Here, the moral problem can be seen to be breaking through again. What happens to these animals will not leave the average human being cold.

The other problem was the industrialization of the landscape. I said that the keeping and using of animals in agriculture was recognized as customary. However, industrialization has breached customary practice so severely that it is difficult to talk of agriculture here at all. In the case of *modern* battery chicken farms and veal fattening stalls one really ought to speak of factories for egg and veal production, the means of production simply being animals.

These two more recent causes of outrage over the behaviour of humans towards animals should be judged somewhat differently to the case of the cab horse. For in the case of cab horses the behaviour concerned was customary for the industry concerned, that of cab drivers. Socially, this occupation is on the threshold of modernity. But biomedical and pharmacological research and the mass farming of animals are entirely modern phenomena. That is to say that we are dealing here with systems of actions which operate independently of the personal attitudes of the people involved, and are dependent on certain professional capabilities which the people working within these systems exercise at certain times. For example, the training of a scientific doctor or a biomedical experimenter contains an explicit training in desensitization.[6] This, however, does not need to embrace the whole person, but can be effective sectorally, that is, within the relevant professional setting.

The social factions we are dealing with in these cases are, on the one hand, groups of people who become angry and commit themselves through personal concern, and, on the other, institutions such as the pharmaceuticals industry or science, which defend their interests and independence. Nevertheless, it can be assumed that, by and large, the representatives of these lobbies or institutions are capable of acknowledging general principles and of reacting with human concern. The main objective of the animal protection law is to regulate the *professional* manner of dealing with animals and bind it to the social consensus concerning the relationship of man to animals. The discourse which led to the formulation and finally the passing of the law was, essentially, an explication and rational justification of the indignation which had been provoked by the modern manner of dealing with animals.

In describing the moral background of this discourse, it is best to start from the result, the principle of the Animal Protection Law[7] as it is formulated in §1:

The objective of this law is to protect the life and well-being of animals on the basis of man's responsibility to animals as fellow-

creatures. No one may cause pain, suffering or damage to an animal
without reasonable grounds. [trans. E.J.]

That no one should cause pain, suffering or damage to an
animal without reasonable grounds was also contained in the
version of 1933. What is new is the reference to the moral background, in the formulation: 'on the basis of man's responsibility to
animals as fellow-creatures'. This formulation has very wide implications, and indicates that the relationship to animals has indeed
now been understood as a serious question, that is, one which
affects our human conception of ourselves. The formulation also
contains a statement of a sameness and a difference which exist
between man and animal. First, the sameness. Humans and animals are fellow creatures. At first sight, one might take this to
express a special regard for animals, in that the formulation
equates them with humans. But that is not the decisive point, and,
in a certain sense, it is not even the case. At any rate, the law does
not state that the animal is something resembling humans; rather,
man is referred to as a creature. This might well be the first time
that this has happened in the whole of German legislation, including the Basic Law. It is true that the Basic Law speaks of the life of
man and of freedom from bodily injury, and the Declaration of
Human Rights speaks of birth and the 'family of man'; nevertheless, up to now the human being's natural being has not been a
theme of law. To the extent that a self-conception of the human
being is expressed in laws and fundamental rights, it is articulated
essentially through terms such as 'person', 'reason', 'freedom' and
'conscience'. On the basis of this conception of the human being,
nature – even the nature that humans themselves are – is for
human beings essentially a tool, an organon, a means, a resource –
that is, it is understood instrumentally. The challenge faced in
arriving at a new consensus regarding the relationship of humans
to animals therefore necessarily called into question the humans'
conception of themselves, and was thus a genuinely moral question. The result is that, in the animal protection law, a self-
conception of humans is inscribed for the first time within the
terms of our legal community, according to which the natural
being of human beings is a part of their essence, and according to
which they are essentially creatures. For this reason they form,
together with animals, the community of creatures.

The term *fellow creature* binds this new self-conception of man to
the Christian tradition. This tradition, unlike the Greek, has actually always recognized a sameness of man and animal in their

creatureliness. The Christian concept of nature, Creation, was not understood, like the Greek term *physis* or the Latin *natura*, in opposition to that which was made by humans, i.e. culture, society, technology, and so on. It was, therefore, not unperceptive to invoke this tradition in the formulation 'fellow creature' in the fundamental clause of the animal protection law; and in the context of a society which, through its history, forms part of the so-called Christian West, it is probably understandable. Nevertheless, this use of the phrase does give rise to a problem. In the context of a state which conceives itself in non-religious terms and in a society which, in principle, is secularized, the reference to a particular religious image of the world is not very useful, since laws are supposed to be neutral in terms of the world-view they reflect, and are binding on members of other religions or on unbelievers. It may be supposed that Jews and Moslems will not have difficulty with the formulation, since they share with Christianity the conception of the world as creation. It is likely to be different for Buddhists. Although they will undoubtedly agree with the content of the provisions of the animal protection law, they will do so for entirely different reasons. Animals are not to be protected because they are the creatures of a god, like ourselves. It is significant that one of the intellectual fathers of the reformulation of the animal protection law plays down the religious content of the wording, noting that creation and creature could also be understood in the sense that we, like animals, are products of creative nature.[8] On the other hand, the religious terminology[9] was not inserted in the wording of the law without a definite intention, since it postulated the *sacredness* or inviolability of living creatures. If people and animals are creatures of God, then they should not be queried or tampered with, which for our time means that they should not be modified genetically. As we have seen, such an appeal to inviolability and holiness is not too remote from the Basic Law. But whether the meaning of *creature* just mentioned has consequences will only be seen from the application of the law, and from new laws and decrees relating to genetic engineering.

The likeness between human beings and animals is a fundamental *topos* of animal protection ethics and, more generally, of bioethical discourse. Usually, however, it is formulated more abstractly and *without* reference to a religious world-view. Albert Schweitzer's principle, quoted earlier, that 'I am life that wants to live, amid life that wants to live', is likely to form the background of most formulations. The link between the bioethical or animal-ethical standpoint and the new self-conception of humans is found here, too. The likeness which Schweitzer stresses lies in the fact that humans, too, are living organisms. It is true that this was recognized in the traditional definition of the *animal rationale*, but there animality was understood as something which, precisely, was *not* essential to humans. This shift in humans' conception of themselves is seen very clearly by Paul W. Taylor in his important book *Respect for Nature. A Theory of Environmental Ethics.*[10] He argues that we humans are members of the terrestrial community of life, and goes on: 'This does not entail a denial of one's personhood. Rather, it is a way of understanding one's true self to include one's biological nature as well as one's personhood' (p. 44). The conclusion to be drawn from what he calls his biocentric world-view is that there is no demonstrable superiority of man over the animal. In this respect, too, the traditional concept of the human being is called into question: 'It is this belief, so deeply and pervasively ingrained in our cultural traditions, that is brought into question and finally denied' (p. 129). The consequence of this for Taylor is that the basic moral attitude towards animals is not responsibility but *respect*, seen as analogous to the respect which persons pay to each other.

Meyer-Abich tries to derive the principle of likeness or equality from the theory of origin. Like animals, we are an outcome of evolution and are therefore related to them in principle.[11] This approach enables him to link equality to inequality, or with degrees of equality. This may be regarded as an advantage, as compared to the rigidity of the equality in Schweitzer and Taylor, which is not dependent on any specific attributes. Meyer-Abich is able to base his account on a ranking of creatures in terms of their proximity to humans, which is well established both scientifically and in everyday experience. This modified concept of equality is pragmatically useful, in addition, because, despite its basically moral attitude towards animals, it allows a good deal of latitude, depending on the rank of the animal concerned. The only trouble-some thing is that this concept seeks to make what is morally permitted towards an animal dependent on intricate anatomical and physiological knowledge based on evolutionary theory.[12] It would be better, as happens in the principal clause of the Animal Protection Law, to postulate a fundamental inequality between human and animal in addition to the equality, but an inequality on a quite different plane.

To formulate this inequality between human being and animal, the Animal Protection Law uses the concept of *responsibility*. This term is, admittedly, an everyday expression and is undoubtedly often misused. But as it appears in the Animal Protection Law it is surely permissible to give it a specific meaning – the one going back to Hans Jonas's analysis of the concept of responsibility.[13] Jonas is a leading exponent of bioethics, and his theories are also a background influence on the re-formulation of the Animal Protection Law. According to Jonas's analysis, the concept of responsibility contains a fundamental asymmetry. Responsibility is not exercised between equals; one is responsible for someone who is dependent, who is in need of help. Jonas's basic model for the concept of responsibility is the parent–child relationship. The parents are responsible for the child because it is helpless without them and depends on their care. The parents' responsibility for the child consists in the fact that they are challenged in a certain way by the neediness of the child. The parents are responsible for the child, but the child is not responsible for the parents – at least, not as long as it is a child.

It is important that this concept of responsibility is based on a relationship of dependence, and not on a specific difference of qualities, skills, resources, etc. In individual cases such a difference will in fact exist, but the concept of responsibility does not relate to it. That is important for the human–animal relationship as well. For it is extremely unfortunate, and counterproductive for the Animal Protection Law, to try to found responsibility on something of which humans have more than animals, such as reason or consciousness. Apart from the fact that there is no scientific basis for denying animals consciousness, such a conception of the inequality between human being and animal would cause one to fall back on the old conception of humanity according to which humans are human to the extent that they differ from animals, by the possession of culture, consciousness and reason. In that case, moreover, the concept of responsibility for animals would take on an almost timeless, cosmological meaning. Some authors do in fact attempt to endow the concept with such a meaning, by interpreting the commandment in Genesis, 'Bring forth abundantly in the earth', to mean that humans have received from God a fundamental responsibility for creation as a whole. It is true that, through genetic engineering, humanity has, or has assumed, a responsibility for the future evolution of the earth. But this example makes it clear that humanity's responsibility for animals, or perhaps for evolution as a whole, *is in no way ahistorical*, but is a consequence of the actual position of power attained by humanity in our century.

Recognition of this actual inequality between human being and animal also underlies the Animal Protection Law. At the present state of technical civilization there are no longer any animals that man cannot control or that could pose a serious threat to him. That was not always the case historically, so that over long periods even of civilized history there was reason for humans to regard animals as enemies or competitors. Just because they had themselves evolved from the animal kingdom it was necessary at that time to conceive of themselves in opposition to animals and to see their essence to lie in not being animals. This conception of the human being has become historically obsolete precisely because humans have become in principle master of all animals.[14] In our century, therefore, humans' conception of themselves is, as a rule, no longer articulated in terms of their difference from animals. It is essential to note this fundamental power of humans over animals because the struggle with nature, and human self-assertion against nature, still continues to govern their existence. Humanity has not mastered the classical natural forces of the four elements – storms, earthquakes, volcanic eruptions and floods – nor has it gained control of micro-organisms. Such organisms are not called animals in the sense used in the Animal Protection Law. Of the organisms which are generally called animals, the rat, at most, is still a genuine enemy to man. It can compete with him in numbers and in the ability to adapt and resist. In the concept of the responsibility of humanity for animals, the Animal Protection Law recognizes the real power relationships and would like to tie human behaviour to these relationships – i.e. to make them patriarchal. Responsibility, therefore, means a duty of care for dependants.

This concept of responsibility is also distinguished by its binding character. If, for example, one wanted to base the inequality between man and animal on the fact that man possesses consciousness while the animal does not, it would not necessarily follow that man needed to take care of animals. But as he has power over animals, he is implicated in their existence from the outset. Finally, this view has the advantage of honesty. The concept of responsibility for animals implicitly acknowledges that man uses them for his purposes. It is therefore unnecessary to posit the relationship of man and animal in principle as one between equals, as is done in utopian ethics – and then to be obliged laboriously to legitimize – by establishing rules of conflict and defining exception – the fact that in individual cases man actually does use animals for his purposes and even kills them. The Animal Protection Law regulates the relations of man to animals as those towards dependants.

This takes us to a further point in the moral debate on animal protection, the question whether it is possible to grant animals explicit rights. Various authors have pointed out that it is entirely feasible to allocate rights to beings who cannot themselves perceive those rights. They argue that this is the case with children and the mentally handicapped, for example.[15] Meyer-Abich has put forward the thesis that it is time to make peace with nature and form a legal community with it. Michel Serres has followed this up with his idea of the natural contract.[16] Now, one must certainly agree with Meyer-Abich that the war with animals is over. But just because animals are in principle subject to humans, we are by no means absolved from the struggle with nature. As far as the animals are concerned, Meyer-Abich would like to see the allocation of rights to animals as part of the Enlightenment programme of emancipation: after the emancipation of slaves, Jews, children and women comes the emancipation of animals.[17] The analogy is flawed, since the power relationships from which the slaves, Jews, children and women were released were laid down by society. The legal equality given to them was, at the same time, the abolition of these power relationships. If one wanted to extend the analogy to animals in this respect, then equality would have to mean that human physical power over them has to be abolished and they have to be given a status like that of cattle in India, which can roam freely. But if the real power relationships are maintained, the granting of rights really amounts to the demand for care, which is already recognized in principle in the Animal Protection Law. Admittedly, the Law is capable of extension in this respect, in that up to now the concept of protection has been understood essentially negatively, i.e. it has the objective of limiting the violence of human beings while imposing hardly any duties of care on them.

If one wanted to install animals themselves as bearers of rights, or establish the legal community advocated by Meyer-Abich, that would nullify what at present can be counted as progress in man's understanding of himself: the fact that his being nature has been incorporated in this understanding. For if one turns animals into legal subjects, they will become socialized, which is to say that they will be assimilated into precisely the form of life which humanity has developed *in contradistinction to* nature, and against his own natural state.

Society's understanding of itself

With this last formulation I have invoked, admittedly, a conception of society which, especially in view of the problems we have with nature, needs to be revised. This takes us to the other example by which I should like to show that the conventions that now need to be negotiated in order to regulate our relationship to nature give rise to genuinely moral problems: these problems are of a kind which causes us to call our current understanding of society into question. As an example, I would mention the new Article 20a of the Basic Law of the Federal Republic of Germany.

> The state also has a responsibility to protect the natural foundations of life for future generations, within the framework of the constitutional order, through legislation and the executive power and the jurisdiction, according to law and justice. [trans. E.J.]

By this article the protection of nature is elevated to a fundamental law, and nature is included among the safeguarded goods enshrined in the Basic Law. To be sure, nature appears here in a limited perspective, a perspective usually called anthropocentric; that is, it is nature in so far as it is the foundation of human life. In other constitutions, such as that of the Free State of Bavaria, nature is set beside cultural monuments – that is, its originality and aesthetic value are also addressed. The crucial thing in our context is that nature protection appears in the Basic Law as a sub-clause of the description of the state in which we live, and, in particular, is formulated as a duty of the state. This in fact represents a fundamental modification of our understanding of society *qua* state. The duties of the state up to now have been to guarantee external and internal security (the security state), to organize and guarantee the legal system (the constitutional state), to organize and promote education (the cultural state), to provide social security for citizens (the social state) and, finally, to manage the economy (the social market economy). The duty of protecting the natural foundations of life is a fundamental modification of the above. For, as can be seen, all the previous duties of the state were *intra-social*, that is, they aimed at regulating and safeguarding the relationships of human beings among themselves. That anything like society and the state were present within nature and were based on nature has up to now played no part in society's conception of itself, as far as this is articulated in the Basic Law. One could speak here, with Günter Altner, of an *oblivion of nature*.[18]

However, this obliviousness towards nature, both in our social self-awareness and in our awareness of ourselves as human beings, is not merely a matter of forgetting; it is a programme. Since the Enlightenment, society has been understood as an organization of human beings created to overcome their dependence on nature and to emancipate themselves from their natural state. In this, nature was quite clearly seen, on one hand, as a basis of life which was unproblematically available for use and, on the other, as a still-preponderant power from which man had every reason to set himself apart. Through the experience of the dialectic of enlightenment or, more generally, of the ambivalence of progress, we have learned that the process of emancipation from nature has placed us only in still greater dependence on nature. Admittedly, the threat emanating from nature today, from the greenhouse effect, the hole in the ozone layer, the erosion and increasing infertility of soils and, finally, the poisoning of the means of life, does not arise from the original nature but from the second nature, anthropogenic nature. From this perspective one would also have to criticize the formulation of Article 20a of the Basic Law. In view of the present condition of nature the formulation is already obsolete, in that what is at stake is no longer just the preservation but the regaining and reproduction of the natural foundations of life. Admittedly, to postulate that as a duty of the state would be to ask too much of the state.[19] The reproduction must be a task for society as a whole, in the sense that while it is a duty of the state it is also a task which must be performed by every social agency, and implicitly must be solved in every production process.[20]

To include nature protection in the catalogue of duties of the state would therefore be only to make a start in incorporating nature in our social understanding of ourselves. Since the terms 'protection' and 'preservation' now fail entirely to match the real demands of the condition of nature which defines our historical situation, and even the term 'development'[21] conveys them only indistinctly and euphemistically, our conception of ourselves as an industrial society must be revised, together with our understanding of social work as the *appropriation of nature for the creation of products*. Some years ago I called for the relationship of production and reproduction to be re-thought by analogy to traditional agriculture.[22] In traditional agriculture the reproduction of nature, i.e. of the field, always enjoyed equal rights alongside the production of goods, i.e. food. Indeed, it can be said that the relationship of

reproduction to production was the reverse of our current understanding of it, in that the real producer was nature while the
farmer's activity was concerned with the reproduction of nature.
Or one might say that production was a joint outcome of the
reproductive work on nature. The present concept of industrial
labour is the exact opposite of this. According to Marx labour was
understood as the appropriation and processing of nature, on the
model of craft work. The productive activity – the forming of
material provided by nature – was allocated essentially to the
worker. It is no wonder that in the course of capitalism and
industrialism nature's part in this production process was overlooked, and in particular, no practical steps were taken to ensure
that nature, on which this process actually depended, was reproduced. This led to the well-known environmental damage. The
Kassel social ecologist Hans Immler has therefore demanded, quite
logically, that 'nature be granted its economic rights'[23] by being
recognized as an essential producer within the industrial process.
'We are the products, nature is the productivity' (p. 76). This
encapsulates in an extreme form the change to our social understanding of ourselves which is prefigured in Article 20a of the
Basic Law.

It has emerged, therefore, that moral problems do actually arise,
and moral argumentation is rightly used, in the discourses which
have led to new conventions in the field of animal and nature
protection, and will lead to others in future. What is called for by
animal and nature protection cannot be delivered without a fundamental revision of our conception of ourselves as human beings
and of our society.

Moral Questions Concerning the Nature We Ourselves Are

Most of the moral questions which are publicly debated arise in
relation to the nature which we ourselves are, that is, with regard
to our bodies and our manner of dealing with life and death. It is
in this area that nature takes on the greatest importance as a
fundamental value of modernity, but from which critical reflection
on modernity also originates. For in this area our understanding of
ourselves as human beings is questioned in principle by the
extraordinary increase in the possibilities of manipulation which

have occurred over the last century. The question which arises is: how much are we still prepared to accept as given – that is, as nature – in the human being. The problems are so diverse and the public discussion so wide-ranging that it is impossible to do justice to all aspects of the moral problems relating to the nature which we ourselves are. It will therefore be necessary to proceed paradigmatically in what follows, using examples to reveal the central problems and the possible strategies for argumentation. All the same, I shall start by giving an overview of the various complexes of problems.

As the first complex I would mention *reproduction medicine* – the whole field from the fertilization of the human ovum to birth. Scientific knowledge and technical possibilities have increased so enormously in this area that there is hardly a process which cannot in principle be understood, controlled and performed technically. A close intertwinement of diagnostic and manipulative methods is found to exist. The human ovum and sperm cell can be isolated and artificial fertilization carried out – *in vitro* fertilization. The extra-uterine cultivation of such a 'fruit' – one can hardly speak of a 'fruit of the womb' any longer – can now be carried forward up to a certain stage, but given the advance of technical developments, it is, of course, foreseeable that production of a human being outside the uterus will be entirely feasible. This opens up, on the one hand, a whole mass of opportunities for research on the human embryo and, on the other, the prospect of diagnosing its predispositions, i.e. carrying out a prenatal analysis of the human genome, with the further prospect of making suitable changes and selections. In particular, surrogate motherhood can be realized in practice, meaning the implantation of an egg fertilized outside the uterus into the uterus of another woman and the growing of the embryo by the latter. Of course, prenatal diagnostics, especially genetic diagnostics, are possible without isolating the egg and sperm cells, by removing cells of the developing embryo from the uterus. From this follows the potential practice of prenatal selection, which is already adopted today to avoid hereditary diseases by induced abortion, and is used in some countries for gender selection. In India, for example, only eighty girls are born for every hundred boys. The capacity for manipulation in this area also extends to the control and management of the birth process itself. The possibility of continuous monitoring of the process and its control by medication and surgery gave rise to the idea of the programmed birth, i.e. a birth meeting a certain ideal standard, or birth by non-indicated Caesarean section. In the United States, for example, one-quarter of all children are already 'brought into the world' by Caesarean section.

The ethical problems which present themselves here can be referred to under the headings of abortion, eugenics, gender selection and surrogate motherhood. But as they call into question the naturalness of the human origin itself, a large number of other *topoi* crystallize around them.

The next complex to be discussed is *gene therapy*. Progress in molecular biology and genetic engineering will sooner or later lead to a situation in which a complete register of the human genome is available. This means that it will be possible to identify the individual components of the human genotype and to know the phenotypic characteristics or procedural functions for which each of them is responsible. Furthermore, it will be possible to dissect, change and reconstruct at will the carrier of hereditary characteristics, DNA. This, of course, opens up for discussion and possible change the constitution of species including humans, as well as the identity of the individual, to the extent that it resides in the uniqueness of his genetic endowment. Moreover, it will be possible to cure genetic defects, and thus hereditary diseases and, finally, to promote the development of individual and species in a particular direction through *improvement* and selection.

Moral questions already arise, of course, in the research required for these developments, in the investigations into life generally and into human life and human embryos in particular. They also arise with interventions in the basic natural make-up, the genetic constitution, of the human being. Here, a distinction must be made between an intervention in the germ line, changes which are passed on to descendants, and an intervention in individual body cells.

The moral questions which arise here can be brought together under the headings of personal identity, species identity, self-determination, responsibility for future generations and, finally, eugenics.

Eugenics in turn forms a complex of its own. The problems of *human breeding*, which have already been posed in connection with traditional animal breeding – the selection of individuals for reproduction and the elimination of unwanted offspring – take on new and greater importance in view of the possibility of genetic manipulation and intervention in the reproductive process.

The fourth complex I would mention is that of *organ transplants*. Progress in surgical and immunosuppression techniques are leading us towards a situation in which practically every organ or part of the human body can be replaced. This, of course, fundamentally changes the relationship of human beings to their own bodies and to bodily identity. But many other morally relevant problems are bound up with this – with regard to organ replacement by artificial devices or by animal organs, for example, or the permissibility of organ removal or, conversely, the duty to make the organs of one's own body available to others. The question arises as to when a person is to be pronounced dead; whether it is permitted to keep him or her vegetally alive after brain death to conserve organs; whether it is permitted to remove organs after death without agreement while alive. In addition, there is the question of a trade in organs, and of the distribution of usable organs for transplants.

As the fifth complex I should like to summarize all the problems connected with *human death*. Here the technical possibilities of extending life have been so far developed that the question arises whether their application to the individual can still be regarded as desirable, and whether death in the context of medical apparatus is worthy of a human being. With regard to organ transplantation the point at issue is at what time a person can be considered actually dead, and whether the demand for the inviolability of the body extends to the cadaver. Finally, there is the problem of euthanasia, of the facilitated death in cases when individuals find life unendurable, or, if they can no longer make themselves understood, whether their lives must be regarded as unendurable in the judgement of doctors or family members.

This sketch of the moral problems which arise in relation to the nature which we ourselves are has not yet been differentiated with regard to the two main branches of ethics; that is, it has not taken account of the difference between the project of a moral life and public moral discourse. Many of the moral questions relating to the nature which we ourselves are must be solved existentially, through the choice and practice of a certain life project. The solutions they entail cannot be generalized, even though they require support from the consensus and the solidarity of people close to the individual concerned. In this section, however, I want to concentrate on the questions which arise in public moral discourse because they call for a consensus on social regulations. For this reason, the first question to be answered is why there is any need for regulation in the sphere of the nature we ourselves are, since there have always been regulations for the social manner of dealing with the human body, with life and death – regulations in the form of medical professional ethics, on the one hand, and existing law, on the other. Why do some of these existing regulations appear inappropriate or inadequate today?

Essentially, there are three answers to this question. Professional medical ethics, institutionalized for so long in the Hippocratic oath,[24] has proved its worth historically. These ethics have been so successful because they represented not only the individual morality of particular doctors but a guild ethics, in that the medical profession ensured their observance. But precisely in this respect they have failed in recent times, notably in the Third Reich, so that self-regulation by the medical profession can no longer be regarded as sufficient in all cases. On the other hand, however, those same events have caused a loss of confidence in legal or state regulation, so that what is needed today is to strengthen both the controls on the state and the possibilities of free self-determination.

Apart from the historical problems concerning medical professional ethics, however, these ethics have also been called into question by the increasing technical capabilities of medicine. In view of the pharmacological and technical possibilities of prolonging life, the fundamental obligation to take measures to preserve life has become questionable. Just because of these measures, together with the growing importance attached to human self-determination – here, that of the patient – the question arises whether the general ban on euthanasia contained in the Hippocratic oath ought to be maintained. These problems have already led to reformulations of the self-imposed obligations of doctors.

The main reason why new social regulations will be needed for our way of dealing with the nature which we ourselves are is that scientific and technical progress has actually given rise to new situations in which the human scope for action has been significantly widened, in particular as a result of gene and transplant technology. These developments put at issue the existing consensus as to what a human being is and what is worthy of a human being, as well as the basic principles of our social co-existence. They impinge partly on the safeguarded goods recognized in the fundamental and human rights, and partly challenge us to define new public goods which need to be safeguarded. Naturally, this needs to be demonstrated with reference to particular cases.

The third area in which there is a need for public regulation is that of research. The new technical methods of dealing medically with the nature we ourselves are arise from, or make necessary, research on the human being, and especially research on human cells and embryos. Such investigations, can, of course, threaten human identity and dignity, and, in some cases, the integrity of the human species. On the other hand, they are protected in principle by the fundamental modern value of freedom of research which is central to our conception of what society is. We are dealing here with a conflict of fundamental rights.

Finally, there is one area which does not call for an extension of social regulation, but rather a reduction. As this represents a special case in relation to the points discussed so far, I should like to deal with it first. It is the problem of abortion, or termination of pregnancy.

Abortion

The debate on §218 of the German Penal Code, which makes abortion a punishable offence, has stirred up the most extensive and dramatic public controversy of the recent past. Apart from many pragmatic and demographic arguments, explicitly moral arguments have been advanced. They are moral in our understanding of the term, since they touch on basic moral conceptions of our culture and on our understanding of society. In going so far as to demand the actual abolition of §218, some of these demands have concerned the legitimacy of state regulations and state intervention in the realm of natural reproduction. But even when they did not go so far, the point at issue has always been a relaxation of an existing social regulation.

The first thing to be clarified, therefore, is what this regulation actually amounts to. The simplest answer is given by its placing in the penal code: *abortion is punishable.* Moreover, the position of this paragraph in the penal code, directly following murder, manslaughter and infanticide, makes it clear that it concerns the protection by criminal law of human life. But that is not quite correct, or at least, not quite adequate. On the one hand, awareness of the *protection of unborn life* as a basic moral theme has only been awakened in the first place by the discussion about §218.[25] Yet its formulation is itself an extension of the basic prohibition on killing, in that it applies to human beings; as we shall see, the question whether and at what time the undeveloped embryo can be referred to as a human being should be left open. On the other hand, however, the placing of this law in the context of the protection of life is inadequate in that, as can be seen from its origin in the Reich Penal Code of 1871, this law forms part of the authoritarian regulation of the whole area of sexual morality or morals in the narrower sense.[26] At that time adultery was still a punishable offence, as were sexual relations between cousins, sexual practices involving animals, homosexuality and the dissemination of pornographic writings. The repeal of all these penal laws signifies a fundamental change in our social conception of ourselves, which can be summed up briefly as the dismantling of the authoritarian state. Today, we *no longer* regard it as a function of the state to supervise the observance of morality in the narrower sense. However, this development has remained incomplete, since the state supervision of individual morality has been retained in form of the compulsory consultation which is a prerequisite for non-criminal abortion. On the other hand, this development has made it possible to isolate and elaborate the theme of the *protection of unborn* life. And it has been strengthened by the need to protect embryos from the interference of scientific research and from genetic manipulation.

The principle that the termination of pregnancy is a punishable offence has been maintained up to now. Any permission to terminate pregnancy is to be seen as an exception. The conditions for making exceptions fall into two main groups, determined by length of pregnancy and by medical or other indications. With regard to length of pregnancy, termination within a specific period is not punishable; with regard to indications, it is not punishable if certain indications for termination are present. Here, a special distinction is made between medical, embryopathic, criminological and emergency indications. Originally, in the fifth Penal Code Reform Law of 1974, the length-of-pregnancy criterion had been established as pragmatically the simplest; the indications criterion was enforced later by a ruling of the Federal Constitutional Court. A particular historical circumstance which still obstructs the debate today is the fact that the period-of-pregnancy criterion had been established in the German Democratic Republic by a law of 1972. Today, a kind of mixture of the time criterion and the indications criterion is operated, with a clear preponderance of the latter. Thus, termination of pregnancy on grounds of indications is not an offence if it takes place within a certain period. It must be noted, however, that no *right* to terminate pregnancy exists and that, in a ruling of 1993, the Federal Constitutional Court did not even permit a termination of pregnancy under certain conditions to be termed *not unlawful*.

This last fact concerning the legal situation makes it clear that we are dealing here with an eminently moral problem, a question of our social understanding of ourselves. This is shown, for example, by a comparison with the legal situation in the United States. There, termination of pregnancy, at least within a certain period, is a *right* covered by the 'right of privacy'.[27] The arguments of the German women's movement, put forward, admittedly, under the somewhat unappealing slogan 'My belly belongs to me', have not led to a social consensus in Germany. To express it differently: it has not been possible to establish the moral *topos* of *self-determination* widely enough to cover a right of parents or of a woman to decide whether she wants to be pregnant or to bring a child into the world. But that was precisely the fundamental maxim of the women who organized themselves in the struggle over §218. I quote the spokesperson of *Aktion §218* at the hearing of the German Bundestag's special committee on reform of the penal code in 1972, Barbara Nirumand. She demanded that it be assumed that 'motherhood and fatherhood must be based on the free decision of the individual, and should not be enforced by the State'. She also noted that it was unrealistic, when reforming the prohibition on abortion, 'not to proceed from the assumption that women are no longer willing to submit to state-enforced birth'.[28] With this formulation Nirumand expressed the reason why the reform of §218 had become a compelling need. Women were actually asserting in huge numbers the right of self-determination demanded by Barbara Nirumand. The number of illegal abortions at that time was estimated at 500,000–2,000,000 per annum. This means that §218 had been subverted in practice – the necessary social consensus had been withdrawn. The maintenance of §218 in force had the further result, of course, that the women concerned were largely dependent on unqualified assistance with abortion, or had their pregnancies terminated abroad.

In our context, which concerns the moral argumentation used in the debate over §218, we can make the following observations at this point: firstly, the moral topos of the *protection of unborn* life has been articulated; and secondly, according to our Basic Law there is no right to privacy or to self-determination. It is true that Article 2 of the Basic Law guarantees the *free development of the personality*; it is true that there are certain protected areas of privacy such as freedom of opinion, freedom of faith and the inviolability of domicile. But that does not mean that a general right of self-determination has been recognized, in face of which the prohibition of abortion would have to be legitimized in certain cases as a restriction of this right. On the contrary, one is obliged to note a general tendency to control step by step by legislation what might be called privacy or the scope for free self-determination. In the case of abortion, however, this is not just a tendency but an historic fact: whenever an act of conception has taken place, the existence of a foetus is no longer a private matter.

Self-determination is a moral *topos* which undoubtedly means more than the *free development of the personality*. The *free development of the personality* is a concept more closely related to education, and could, at most, call for an additional *field of application* for the realization of the personality. Self-determination, by contrast, articulates an independence from tutelage and 'leading by the nose', it implies a freely projected life and independence of judgement and decision in particular situations. For this reason self-determination is less a humanistic term than a *topos* of emancipation and of liberation movements in general. In the Declaration of Human Rights the concept appears as the right of peoples to self-determination. The abolition of §218 was a goal relating to self-determination in the struggle of women for emancipation and equal rights.

The establishment of the *topos* of the *protection of unborn life* was, in a sense, easier, as is was introduced, on the one hand, to legitimize a social consensus already canonized, that is, §218, and, on the other, because it was effectively assisted by other threats to human life from science and technology. Nevertheless, the legitimizing of this *topos*, and thus the retrospective justification of §218, were still difficult, since to legitimize human life from the moment of its conception, i.e. before one could speak of a sentient being, before it was endowed with interest and could be addressed as a person, and long before birth, with which it first becomes an organically independent entity in the world – to legitimize this proved a difficult task. In the analysis of the legal philosopher Norbert Hoerster, such legitimization is really only possible if the value to be protected is not tied to some empirical quality of the developing organism which may be present at this or that stage, but to a transcendental attribute, namely its likeness to God. He invokes the joint declaration of the Council of Evangelical Churches in Germany and of the German Conference of Bishops of 1989 in asserting that 'each human individual, when it comes into being, is endowed by God with an immortal soul and is thus made in His likeness'.[29]

Leaving aside the question whether this assertion is theologically tenable, it is certainly a moral *topos*, since it concerns the self-understanding of the human being and undoubtedly forms part of the background of the moral culture which gave rise to §218. The question is only whether this context is still an appropriate basis for our social understanding of ourselves. The fundamentally secular and lay character of our society and our state argue against this. It is, no doubt, especially significant that this idea was put forward precisely by a Catholic moral theologian in the debate over §218. I quote Professor Anselm Hertz, OP:

> The theory concerning the soul, predicated on a specific world-view, would be rejected in the juridical sphere with the argument that conceptions based on world-views are without legal relevance in a pluralistic society. Only a general consensus on the intrinsic value of human life can decide on the need to protect nascent life, thereby making it a value to be safeguarded and thus a legal good. In this case nascent human life would have to be included within the protection of legal goods, as it would be illogical to seek to protect human life but not nascent human life.[30]

This states clearly that we are concerned here with society's understanding of itself: we live in a secular and pluralist society. For this reason social regulations cannot be legitimized by world-views held only by certain religious sections of society. Instead of doing that, the theologian just quoted tries to invoke a different basis for consensus, that of reason, by using the catchword 'illogical'.

Still more important is the fact that in his argumentation he sets aside the historical basis of §218 which was mentioned earlier – the unity of law and morality. Here, he invokes St Thomas Aquinas:

> St Thomas Aquinas deals with the question whether it is the task of human, i.e. positive law to prohibit all human wrongdoing and place it under threat of punishment. He answers in the negative: only serious human wrongdoing deserves punishment. He justifies this with two considerations: firstly, only wrongdoing which causes damage to others should be penalized, since without this prohibition human society could not survive. Murder and theft are mentioned as examples. Secondly, only wrongdoing from which the majority is able to abstain should be punishable.[31]

Against this background, the theologian quoted could actually argue for the abolition of §218. At any rate, with St Thomas Aquinas he formulates an extremely modern, or rather, a current conception of state and society, according to which the institutionalized, i.e. legal order of social life does indeed have a moral foundation, but does not use it to assert morality. This brings us back to the beginning of our investigation. With the principle of the general criminality of abortion, §218 perpetuates the authoritarian model of the state.

Genetic engineering

Genetic research and engineering are a characteristic example of the way in which social regulations can become necessary because possibilities of human action have outstripped the capacity of the existing set of customary practices, laws and more general moral ideas to cope with them. That genetic research and engineering pose moral questions when they concern the human genome is self-evident: the integrity of both the individual person and the human species is at stake. Ethical discussion of research on human beings and on the use of possible genetic engineering techniques began at an early stage – early enough in this case – before the specific techniques were really successful and marketable. Günther Anders's thesis that human expertise has run far ahead of moral development does not apply in this case. On the contrary, a large number of self-constraints on doctors and researchers already exist, as well as legal regulations.[32] In Germany, for example, there is a law protecting the embryo; a ban on genetic code therapy has been written into the Swiss constitution, and a similar regulation is contained in the Austrian law on reproductive medicine.[33] All these legal provisions rule out any intervention in genetic material which could have an effect on subsequent generations. Furthermore, a UNESCO declaration on bioethics and a bioethical convention of the Council of Europe are currently under discussion.[34] All these regulations and legal resolutions are largely driven by the anticipation of possible dangers. Nevertheless, they also contain the first signs of a new basic moral consensus with regard to the nature we ourselves are. It is therefore worthwhile to explore the implications of these early signs, particularly as they have not yet taken on any fixed form and could be undermined by *successes* of genetic engineering. This can be seen in a prominently placed formulation in the preamble of the draft of the UNESCO declaration on bioethics. It states that the declaration has come into being in recognition of the fact that 'research on the human genome and the resulting applications open up vast prospects for progress in improving the health of individuals and of humankind as a whole'.

These hopes in human progress through science and technology – positively naive[35] in face of our experiences with the project of modernity – give grounds to fear that despite regional and medi-cal-professional restraint with regard to the human genome, some-where development in genetic engineering will be carried forward with all possible brutality. In the long term, this situation could lead to a fragmentation of the human species. It is therefore all the more important to agree on what *we* wish to understand by being human.

I should like to point out the most important ethical aspects of this question with reference to three central problems: firstly, germ-line gene therapy; secondly, the possibilities of eugenics through genetic engineering, and thirdly, the problems arising from the introduction of genetic mapping or a genetic register for personal and social life.

At present there is agreement that genetic engineering methods can be used for illnesses caused by genetic factors, as long as they involve somatic therapy and do not influence the genetic germ-line. A somatic therapy is one which is applied only to the cells or stem cells of the affected organ of an adult person. It is compared to chemotherapy or transplant therapy and in Germany is held to be safeguarded by the law governing the manufacture and pre-scription of medicines. Germ-line gene therapy, by contrast, is morally problematic and is actually prohibited. It would intervene in the DNA of the stem cells before or immediately after fertiliza-tion, with the result that the change produced would be hereditary. That germ-line gene therapy is so widely, indeed almost univer-sally, proscribed seems at first sight paradoxical. For if one wants to make an impact on hereditary illnesses, then surely it is desir-able to eliminate the responsible genetic defect permanently. How-ever, the rejection of this therapy is understandable in view of the mass of counter-arguments and problems. There are numerous pragmatic considerations, such as the fact that to develop the necessary techniques research on embryos would be needed, that experiments with this technology could actually cause genetic defects, and, finally, that this whole direction of research would inaugurate a genetic eugenics. The last argument could turn out to be non-pragmatic, i.e. an argument of principle. I shall come back to that. It is all the more important to consider the categorical, or, as I call them, the moral arguments, just because it may well be that the present consensus which rejects germ-line gene therapy is based mainly on pragmatic considerations.

In moral argumentation important new moral *topoi* are now emerging, which point towards a new human self-understanding and give new content to the concepts of personal integrity and human dignity. These are the *topoi* of the essentially *natal* and *natural* character of human origin. These *topoi* were probably first developed in the report of the commission of enquiry on 'Opportunities and risks of genetic engineering' of 1987. They have special and far-reaching implications in a number of ways. For example, to legitimize embryo research and germ-line gene manipulation it is often argued that these are done before any person who could be a bearer of human dignity has come into being. Against this, by introducing the topoi of the 'natal' and 'natural' character of origin, the concept of human beings is so formulated that their provenance from nature, and thus the provenance of the person from nature, and therefore the person's facticity and contingency, are an integral part of this concept. That early manipulation of the heritable material could impair the self-understanding, the self-respect and therefore the dignity of the person who develops later has been very aptly expressed by Hermann Schmid. In his report on *Gentherapie aus juristischer Sicht* (Gene therapy from a legal perspective), he writes: 'Children ought not to exist as the products of their parents and their doctors. All should have the possibility of understanding themselves and their essence as an expression of a fate which lies outside the human sphere – or is created by God – and not as the project and the more or less successful experiment of other people' (p. 142). This attempt to incorporate the natural origin of human beings in their dignity is supplemented by an endeavour to establish a right to individuality and imperfection. Underlying this is an awareness not only that individuality is threatened by the possible technology of cloning, but that it is already called into question by genetic manipulation in relation to a *norm*. The linking of the right of individuality to a right of imperfection is, no doubt, one of the most fundamental protests made against the project of modernity under the banner of nature. For the fact that humanity has become its own project, and the improvement of the human being its programme, is one of the four main tendencies of the whole project of modernity.[36] I quote from the 'Benda Report', in which these *topoi* were probably articulated for the first time:

> Both his unique individuality and his imperfection have always been part of the essence of the human being. To measure humans against an allegedly correct norm and to manipulate them genetically to match this norm would be to contradict the image of the human being in the Basic Law and to violate human dignity in the deepest possible way.[37]

The observation that the acceptance of one's own imperfection, and indeed, a right of imperfection, are an intrinsic part of human dignity and self-respect may be one of the most significant moral advances made in the current debate on gene therapy. But how little this *topos* has been accepted up to now can be seen from objections to the prohibition of germ-line gene therapy put forward by Hermann Schmid. He maintains, for example, that 'far from violating human dignity, gene therapy, by restoring health, would make it possible in the first place'. Furthermore, one should bear in mind 'that grave but avoidable illness cannot be seen as constitutive of the personal identity of a human being'.[38]

This argument founders on a problem to which Schmid himself draws attention – the difficulty of deciding to what the concept of human dignity refers: to the individual or to the species. For the individual human being, dignity is not established by eliminating a genetic defect, since he or she did not exist before the genetic manipulation was carried out. On the other hand, if he or she does exist, then a grave illness is indeed constitutive of the identity of a human being. On this question the moral philosopher Christoph Rehmann-Sutter, who specializes in genetic ethics and opposes a concept of health based on the ideal of perfection, remarks aptly: 'Is not true health rather a strength, a capability? An ability to deal with imperfection, and that means with mourning, suffering and death?'[39] For the self-understanding and self-respect of individual human beings it is undoubtedly of extreme importance whether or not they must see themselves as a product of manipulation. It is even decisive for the self-understanding of each individual human being whether the human genome is regarded as inviolable or is made available for manipulation. For in the latter case, even if no manipulation has taken place in an individual case, the human being would have to regard himself or herself as in principle an artefact. On this point I quote Christoph Rehmann-Sutter:

> Germ-line gene therapy involves crossing a boundary beyond which lies the specific technical manipulation of the human genotype. This boundary is extremely significant, not so much because I believe this intervention to be forbidden *in principle* for us humans, but because crossing it changes something quite fundamental in the relationship we humans adopt to our own imperfection and to the imperfection of others. The mere fact that we influence the structure of the human genome at a certain point deprives it of the character of a natural disposition and gives it that of an artefact . . . But it then has the status of an artificial product not only at the point where

changes have actually been made, but also where none have been made. For not to make changes is also a decision which henceforth must be attributed to human beings.[40]

This leads on to the second area of problems, which I have mentioned under the general heading of genetic eugenics. These explicitly concern the question of improving human beings understood in the sense of the human species. At present there is undoubtedly no universal consensus on this question, as the preamble to the UNESCO declaration on bioethics has already shown. This lack of consensus became explicitly obvious when the topic of which eugenic practices were to be banned was dropped from the UNESCO Declaration in the last stage before its adoption by the General Conference of November 1997. Why, it might be argued, should one not want to improve humankind genetically? Is not the desire for perfection actually self-evident? Does not wanting something always mean wanting something better? In face of such arguments it is hardly enough to point out that one would not know in which respects humankind was to be perfected, or whether an improvement in one respect – in long-term memory or intelligence, for example – really was a step forward.

Nevertheless, the UNESCO declaration does introduce a new moral *topos* which might provide support for a ban on genetic eugenics. Article 1 of the Declaration concludes by stating that 'the human genome . . . is the heritage of humanity'.

This concept is certainly still very indefinite, but because other things have already been declared to be part of the common heritage of humankind, it does imply certain statements. For example, the seabed, the moon, together with books, works of art and historical monuments in general, have been declared part of the human heritage, and likewise all cultures in their diversity and as a totality. Such statements mean that a good declared to belong to the human heritage may not be particularized, that is, may not be appropriated by individual groups or states. It must in principle be available to all. We have here, therefore, a kind of return to the idea of common land, but on the plane of humanity. What might this idea imply with regard to the human genetic material and its possible manipulation? I believe that it implies that products of the genetic manipulation of humans may not be patented, as has already been done for animals and threatens by analogy to be done for humans. Further, this idea is likely to imply that each human being or each human group may not regard *its* genetic material as its property, but must feel itself to be a component of humankind – as is actually the case through the ramifications of kinship. From this it would follow, at least, that each genetic manipulation of the germ-line would require a practically universal legitimation. It would be quite out of the question to carry out improvements according to *particular* desiderata.

However, these considerations show implicitly how weak this level of opposition is in face of the idea of improving humankind. By contrast, the historical argument against eugenics is strong. The Europe-wide ban on germ line gene therapy is no doubt crucially affected by this argument. In the 1989 guidelines of the German medical profession on gene therapy any *positive intervention* with regard to genetic material is ruled out. The historical reason for the rejection of eugenics lies in the experience of the so-called Third Reich. In National-Socialist Germany the idea of a scientific eugenics, which had already come into being, was brought together with a racist anthropology.[41] It would be an understatement to argue today that the National Socialists misused scientific eugenics. Certainly, that is also the case, in the sense that what they regarded as unfit to live was *eradicated* in the name of eugenics. The danger of such misuse would in itself justify a ban on eugenic measures. But that could hardly be called a moral justification. Such a justification would spring, rather, from the reality of the link between eugenics and racism. The so-called Third Reich itself expounded this link, and its possibility seems unavoidable. It consists in the fact that the question as to what constitutes a *good human being* is answered from the perspective of a particular group. This would run deeply counter to our basic understanding of society with regard both to the equality of human beings and to the fundamental pluralism of society.

We have here an example of a case in which the historical context fundamentally determines the moral discourse, at least for us. We would call into question our historical understanding of ourselves if we did not take account of experiences from our past. Equally, the argument has shown that these experiences are generalizable in terms of their consequences. It is interesting to note that an historical argument relevant to us plays a part in the American debate on euthanasia. The American professor of ethics, Tom L. Beauchamp, for example, writes:

> It therefore seems sensible to discard at the outset any such distinction [between justified and unjustified euthanasia], to prevent the inevitable slide into a situation devoid of principles. With regard to the historical context, it should be pointed out that precisely this has

happened in the darker phases of human history – including the period of the Nazi regime, when euthanasia was first practised with the best intentions in the case of very seriously handicapped non-Jewish Germans, and the programme was gradually extended to all persons classified as harmful to the race.[42]

I come, finally, to the topic which I mentioned under the heading of gene analysis, genetic mapping and genetic registration. The possibility of a more-or-less complete genetic analysis of the individual harbours many dangers which necessitate social regulations. For example, the privacy of a person is threatened by the possible use of genetic information on that person, and presents a danger of discrimination – in the labour market, for example. Moreover, a person's self-understanding cannot be untouched by the fact that he 'knows the truth about himself' genetically. It is therefore highly significant that the UNESCO declaration contains the following passage: 'Everyone has a right to respect for their dignity and for their rights regardless of their genetic characteristics. That dignity makes it imperative not to reduce individuals to their genetic characteristics and to respect their uniqueness and diversity' (Article 2). One might, to an extent, welcome the recognition that the radical individuality of each human being – which actually is only postulated – also has its *fundamentum in re*, in that each person is indeed a unique entity according to his or her genetic material. However, this knowledge does, of course, carry the danger that the individuality of a human being might be reduced to this very fundament. An early form of this can be seen in the use of genetic fingerprinting in crime detection. Here, the dignity of the human being actually has to be protected *against* its natural substrate. A crucial aspect of human self-understanding lies in not allowing oneself to be reduced to one's genetic identity but – to mention the alternatives – to regard identity as something achieved throughout life, a biographical product.

To achieve this, it might even be necessary to close one's eyes to one's own genetic dispositions. For it is only too easy – as classical tragedies teach us – for an oracle to take control of a biography. In his book *Mensch nach Maß* (Humans made to measure) Wolfgang van den Daele even talks of a right of ignorance.[43] As we shall see in a moment, such a right has been adopted in the Council of Europe's convention on bioethics. However, whether or not one wants to make use of that right forms part of the project of a moral existence.

For social discourse on the admissibility of genetic analysis and the possible use of such data in social life, however, the danger of discrimination must be considered. If such methods were to be permitted at all, then a decision not to submit oneself to genetic examination could lead to negative discrimination – for example, in job applications. It is therefore to be welcomed that the right to preserve the private sphere with regard to genetic information is mentioned in the Council of Europe's convention on bioethics.

> Article 10 (Private life and right to information): Everyone has the right to respect for private life in relation to information about his or her health. Everyone is entitled to know any information collected about his or her health. However, the wishes of individuals not to be so informed shall be observed. In exceptional cases, restrictions may be placed by law on the exercise of the rights contained in the preceding paragraph in the interests of the patient.

The next paragraph is explicitly directed against discrimination:

> Article 11 (Non-discrimination): Any form of discrimination against a person on grounds of his or her genetic heritage is prohibited.

What really follows from this stipulation is that genetic analysis for any other than therapeutic purposes should not be performed at all, and that its results may only be used in the therapeutic context.

This brings to an end the account of the second area in which moral questions arise with regard to the nature we ourselves are. A discussion of prosthetic technologies and transplant possibilities would yield analogous results. Moral questions arise in all these areas because what is to be regarded as nature in us humans, and therefore what our being a part of nature actually means for our understanding of ourselves as humans, is made a matter for debate and possible modification. It is emerging that the very possibility of its technical manipulation is making the nature we ourselves are into a central moral *topos*.

Moral Problems in Dealing with Foreigners

There is hardly a single area of social behaviour of which the regulation more profoundly determines the kind of society we live in than the way in which we deal with foreigners. The reason is that this behaviour is directly dependent on the definition of belonging and not-belonging, on how this distinction is made and on the mediation between the groups thus separated. Just as my conception of the other and my relationship to others define my own understanding of myself, our social understanding of ourselves is crucially shaped by our way of perceiving foreigners and our relationship to them. Questions about the regulation or our behaviour towards foreigners are therefore serious questions, and thus moral ones.

In Germany, the discourse on foreignness and our relationship to foreigners has been shaped, on the one hand, by the historical perspective – the racial policies of the so-called Third Reich, the expulsion and, finally, the annihilation of Jews and gypsies – and, on the other, by the present situation. In Germany today the relationship to foreigners is no longer, or not only, an external relationship, but an internal one. The German population includes about seven million foreigners – roughly 10 per cent. They are referred to as 'aliens', although for the most part they, and often their parents, were born in Germany and in most cases have lived in Germany for decades. On one hand, the high proportion of aliens in the German population is maintained artificially, since it is made extraordinarily difficult for them to obtain citizenship, while, on the other, it is continuously reproduced by the arrival of more and more foreigners, primarily asylum-seekers – about 100,000 annually. This gives rise to two main topics for the public debate on how to deal with foreigners: first, the controversy over citizenship and secondly, the right of asylum. These are debates in which explicit regulation – laws and rights – are at issue. However, they are often carried on in a climate of hostility to foreigners and of racism, and this gives us cause to ask about our customary behaviour towards foreigners in a more comprehensive sense. This will lead us back, at the end of the book, to the question of customary behaviour in general. Even though *all* public moral discourses are concerned with customary behaviour, it is especially clear in this case that there is a striking lack of customary behaviour with regard to foreigners, or that what is customary is urgently in need of change. There appears to exist a need for society to make up lost ground in learning how to behave towards foreigners, without which there is hardly any prospect of reaching satisfactory solutions in the political debate about legal regulations.

The right of citizenship

The main reason for the large proportion of members of our society who are not citizens in the full sense (8.9 per cent in 1997) is the high hurdle placed in the way of naturalization. In addition, hostility to foreigners and cultural intolerance help to ensure that the foreigners in the German Federal Republic depend strongly on support from their compatriots, cut themselves off in ghetto-like communities and, as a reaction to their hostile environment, often do not want to be naturalized.

The German law of citizenship does not really fit a modern state, in that it attributes citizenship but makes it practically impossible to acquire it;[44] it is a *lex sanguinis* and not a *lex solis*, which means in effect that one becomes a German citizen by virtue of German blood, that is, by descent. Admittedly, since 1 January 2000 it has also been possible to obtain German citizenship through having been born in Germany.[45] The preconditions are that one parent has had his or her legal domicile in the Federal Republic of Germany for at least eight years and has a right of residence or has held an unlimited residence permit for the last three years. However, this first step towards a *lex solis* is highly ambivalent, since the children concerned can also obtain the nationality of their parents on the basis of their parents' nationality. For this reason §29 of the Law of Citizenship withdraws the concession to the children of foreign parents by requiring them to decide on one nationality by the age of twenty-three. If they fail to do so, German citizenship is automatically forfeited. For this reason the legal expert Helmut Rittstieg describes this kind of citizenship as 'dissolvently conditional' (*auflösend bedingt*) and observes critically that 'Germans with lesser rights in relation to Germans by descent' are being created (*Deutsches Ausländerrecht*). This form of natural acquisition of German citizenship is, therefore, a half-hearted but nevertheless welcome step towards a revision of the relationship of Germans to their aliens – and thus implicitly towards a revision of the conception of what it means to be German.

For adults, the acquisition of German citizenship remains extraordinarily difficult. Only since 1993 has a right of naturalization for foreigners existed in some cases. According to the new version of the law regarding foreigners, in force since 1 January 2000, an alien 'who has legally had his or her principal residence in Germany for eight years' [trans. E.J.] has the right of naturalization

(§85). This only applies, however, under additional conditions, two of which are very rigorous. Firstly (§85.3), foreigners must be able 'to earn a livelihood for themselves and family members entitled to support without claiming welfare and unemployment benefit'; secondly (§85.4), they must 'relinquish or forfeit their previous nationality' [trans. E.J.]. The clause just quoted, §85.3, excludes from citizenship all socially disadvantaged people, such as the unemployed or unemployable, and, in particular, it prevents asylum-seekers from obtaining the right of naturalization simply by remaining in the country.

The requirement that the applicant lose or relinquish his or her previous citizenship is also very drastic, since, on the one hand, it represents an imposition on the person concerned – since they are forced to give up a part of their identity – and on the other, because very many states do not release their citizens in this way, or not easily. According to German law there is, as a rule, no possibility of dual nationality.

It is true that under some circumstances, as specified in §85, multiple nationality is accepted, but in individual cases it will be extremely difficult to prove that these conditions – for example, that 'the foreign state regularly refuses to release its citizens' (§87.2, trans. E.J.) – are fulfilled.

There is no direct way to obtain German citizenship – that is, no law of immigration. German citizenship can only be obtained if the applicant has already, through other constellations and opportunities, met the essential conditions – legal domicile and secure livelihood – while still a foreigner. Moreover, the right to be naturalized even under these conditions has only been achieved through very laborious political compromises. The consensus on the matter is still unstable and could easily break down if there is a shift in the political climate or a change of government. The possibilities of obtaining German citizenship remain in strong contrast to what is customary in other European countries, such as France, the United Kingdom, the Netherlands and Sweden. In all these countries a five-year period of residence is, as a rule, sufficient and, above all, those born in the country have the right of citizenship without restriction – i.e., a *lex solis* obtains.

The question of German citizenship and of the rules and laws governing naturalization is, indeed, crucial for our society's conception of itself. Because citizenship is *really* based on the blood relationship, the racial idea – that is, the idea that race constitutes the basis and unity of the state – is preserved, blocking the way to a modern conception of the state and a renewal of society's understanding of itself in contradistinction to that of the Third Reich. In their book *Heimat Babylon*, Daniel Cohn-Bendit and Thomas Schmid rightly point out that at the time of the emergence of the nation state, in the late eighteenth and early nineteenth centuries, Germans were seeking, and found, in race (*das Volk*) the cement which would bind together the many petty states making up Germany at that time, and overcome the regionalism and particularism that went with them:

> From that time onwards there was in Germany (and especially among its elites, an increasing tendency to make 'the others' – the French, the English, the Jews, the non-residents – responsible for all problems. In short, because the nation state was founded not on political but on racial concepts, and thus on hostility to foreigners, and because this form did not suit the Germans, it took a chauvinistic turn.[46]

Consequently, the concept 'German' still has racist traits; that is to say, one simply cannot imagine a German who is black or of Asiatic appearance.

The discussion on the basis of citizenship, dual nationality and naturalization therefore always revolves around the way in which we wish to understand our state community and in what sense it is called German.

There is a further problem connected to the right of citizenship – the question of the sense in which, and how self-consistently, our society is democratic. The high proportion of foreign citizens in the Federal Republic means that a significant part of the population is excluded from democratic rights of participation, since the right to vote depends on citizenship. The foreign citizens are under all the obligations which apply to the regular citizens. They also share their general rights and can, as a rule, make use of the welfare state; *yet* they are not involved in the formation of the political will and they cannot be elected. Their interests could therefore, at most, be represented for them by committed German citizens. A fundamental principle of democracy, that all those who have reached majority can take part in the decisions which affect them, is set aside. It is self-evident that there can be no consensus of society as a whole on this point, and that the maintenance of the convention of restricted rights of participation can only be repressive.

The right of asylum

The right of asylum, as originally contained in Article 16 of the Basic Law, was unique and exemplary world-wide. The second clause states succinctly: 'No German may be extradited to a foreign country. Persons persecuted for political reasons enjoy the right of asylum' [trans. E.J.]. The last sentence is unique because it grants to a non-citizen who is seeking protection a *right*, and does not merely formulate an obligation of the state to give asylum. Moreover, this right of asylum is *absolute*, in the sense that it is not dependent on a particular political situation, or on a policy of the German state, and is not granted in relation to certain countries and regimes. In the debates of the Herrenchiemsee Constitutional Convention, and of the Parliamentary Council, this point was given special prominence by fears that the right of asylum might be claimed by 'refugees with undemocratic inclinations'.[47]

What induced the Herrenchiemsee Convention and the Parliamentary Council to incorporate asylum as an absolute right in the Basic Law was, clearly, the experience of the Third Reich. Even in the current debate on the right of asylum it is constantly argued that Germany has a moral obligation to grant asylum because it itself had repressive regimes at the time of the Third Reich and again in the GDR, which made refugees of many of its citizens and forced them to seek asylum in other countries. However, this historic obligation towards the 'free world', in which hundreds of thousands of Germans found shelter, is only one side of the historical background of the debate. The other side is that the German emigrants were by no means everywhere received with open arms, were frequently faced with closed borders and were sent back even when their lives were at risk. In face of the influx of refugees and the political situation, the conditions on which foreigners were admitted were tightened in the countries concerned. In his book *Emigration. Die Geschichte der Hitler-Flüchtlinge 1933–1945* the human-rights activist Kurt R. Grossmann writes:

> When the racial persecution was at its height, states sent back women and children, and even women in an advanced state of pregnancy. From at least 1938 democratic countries such as the United Kingdom, Sweden and Denmark adopted a policy of repatriating refugees who crossed their border without a visa. But entry visas could only be obtained after lengthy formalities. Illegal immigration remained a punishable offence – a hopeless contradiction in

face of the mortal danger from which political and racial refugees were trying to escape.[48]

Against the background of such experiences, there were strong reasons to formulate a *right* of asylum for refugees. The discussions of the past years have been essentially concerned with restricting this right, or with legitimizing the actual restriction with further provisions, in particular, the law on asylum procedure of 1982.

Today, when a large part of the population and the decisive political faction would like to be rid of the law of asylum, the Geneva Convention on Refugees of 1953, extended in 1969, plays a significant role.[49] For it lays down in terms of international law – sanctioned by about 100 states – certain minimum requirements to be met by asylum regulations, which it would be difficult for the German Federal Republic to disregard without loss of international standing. According to Article 1, Paragraph 2 of the Geneva Convention on Refugees, a refugee is defined as a person who 'owing to a well-founded fear of being persecuted for reasons of race, religion, nationality, membership of a particular social group or political opinion, is outside the country of his nationality'.[50] The crucial provision is found in Article 33, which proclaims a ban on expelling and sending back refugees:

> No Contracting State shall expel or return a refugee in any manner whatsoever to the frontiers of territories where his life or freedom would be threatened on account of his race, religion, nationality, membership of a particular social group or political opinion.[51]

As I said, this formulation sets minimum standards; on the other hand, it falls short of the German law on asylum in that it only prohibits expulsion and sending back, but does not grant the refugee a right of entry. According to the German asylum law, in principle, a foreigner who is persecuted politically could make an application for asylum even from outside German territory, or, conversely, the German state should allow anyone who wants to claim asylum to enter the country.

As mentioned earlier, this right has already been substantially restricted by the law on asylum procedure of 1982. According to Article 16 of the Basic Law, the right of asylum cannot, strictly speaking, be denied to anyone, and this, as a fundamental right, cannot be affected by changes to the constitution. That is why it was decided to use the alternative method of raising a procedural wall against asylum. The procedure now requires the refugee to provide proof of persecution. It also acts as a practical deterrent to the seeking of asylum by imposing compulsory accommodation and thus splitting up families, by maintaining long waiting times, and so on. The right of asylum, already extensively undermined in this way, has now been taken practically *ad absurdum* by an addition to Article 16 of the Basic Law. According to it, no one may now claim asylum who enters either from other states of the European Community or from states 'in which it appears to be guaranteed by the legal situation, the application of law and the general political conditions that neither political persecution nor inhumane or degrading punishment takes place' (Basic Law, Art. 16a, §3). Which states these are is determined by a law, and can therefore be subject to the political judgement of other states. As the Federal Republic is now surrounded by a cordon of such states, asylum-seekers can only reach the country by sea, by air or by illegal means. In practice the number of asylum-seekers has been kept constant by these measures, and the originally *absolute* right of asylum has been abolished.

The currently sanctioned consensus regarding the treatment of foreigners seeking protection has now been described. This consensus is supported by a broad political majority – without which the change in the constitution would not have been possible. It cannot be said, however, that the problem has been solved by this so-called compromise on asylum, or that the debate on asylum in the population has been laid to rest. On the contrary, repeated scandalous expulsions made on the basis of the present legal situation constantly cause the debate to flare up again and give rise to resistance going as far as civil disobedience and illegal actions.

Our conception of the society we want to live in does indeed depend on the regulations concerning the right of asylum. This can be seen in the fact that the right has been called generous or over-generous. At the time of the Cold War the Federal Republic of Germany was rather emphatic in seeing itself as a free constitutional state, and, priding itself on this status, accepted a large number of refugees – who, admittedly, were largely 'brothers and sisters' from the 'so-called' German Democratic Republic. Today, our understanding of ourselves as a free state still depends on our readiness to accept political refugees. This self-evaluation is endangered if, driven either by the hostility to foreigners in our own population or by purely pragmatic considerations about our capacity to accept refugees or the social burden they represent, we restrict the right of asylum. Political freedom itself suffers if one is unwilling to share it with others. And any quibbling about the right of asylum threatens our historical awareness. The willingness in effect to abolish Article 16 of the Basic Law by an addendum has caused a break with the past, a repression of the historical origin of the Federal Republic. The experience of flight and persecution in the Third Reich simply does not admit a purely pragmatic modification of a right as fundamental as that of asylum.

In the debate on the right of asylum it is constantly argued that the primary objective is to curb the misuse of the right and to distinguish genuine political refugees from those who wish to enter the Federal Republic for merely economic reasons. It should not be overlooked here, however, that for political refugees, the Federal Republic is also especially attractive, in the spectrum of possible destination countries, because of its economic prosperity. If one wishes to neutralize this factor in one way or another, that is itself a serious question, in that the Federal Republic is not willing to share its wealth with at least a part of the rest of the world, and especially with those who enter its territory as refugees. In that case our social understanding of ourselves is not determined by generosity, but more and more by a siege mentality.

Customary behaviour towards foreigners

The right of asylum, however admirably conceived by the fathers of the Basic Law, never had a broad basis of support among the population. As long as the East–West confrontation existed the praxis of asylum was straightforward, as anyone who knocked on our door could be celebrated as a triumph of the Free World and the western way of life, and a defeat for totalitarianism. Statistics on numbers of refugees were therefore published and read with satisfaction. But this did not reflect an openness towards foreigners or a willingness to integrate them. On the contrary, one is obliged to note a long-standing tradition of hostility to foreigners, and an inability to uphold courteous relations with them. For this reason, the present discourse on dealing with foreigners is not concerned merely with formal regulations, such as the rights of citizenship and asylum, but with a *culture* of the treatment of foreigners, that is, with the customary behaviour and the social attitudes and assumptions which need to be mediated by education.

That there is a prospect of change in this area is shown by the practical discourse on external nature. Here, an environmental ethics has come into being which concerns the treatment of resources such as refuse and packaging, and relates generally to consumer habits and tourism. This discourse has actually led to new forms of customary behaviour which are successfully mediated by education, and especially by schools. Just as there is now an environmental education, one should aim also at a multicultural education. How much any such thing is lacking becomes strikingly apparent if one peruses the classic works on good behaviour in search of a category on 'behaviour towards foreigners'. The standard work by Knigge, for example, gives advice on behaviour towards practically every conceivable human category – superiors, princes, people in love, poor people, scholars, etc., etc. But guidance on behaviour towards foreigners is not to be found, any more than it is in Salzmann's primer on morals.

If one looks back in history, one can observe an increase in the rights of foreigners and, concurrently, a decrease in personal courtesy towards them. Originally, in the legal arrangements of antiquity, the foreigner or stranger was without rights. The law related only to the members of the community concerned. However, the stranger was under the protection of Zeus and, in the individual case, enjoyed personal hospitality. Within a community, therefore, the stranger was protected as the guest of a particular person or family. The right of hospitality was itself a highly developed institution, governing many matters concerned with acting as host, showing respect, presenting oneself and exchanging gifts. In the long run it created personal links which in some cases had political consequences. In particular, trade relationships gave rise to a body of law on strangers. In Greek communities there were *synoecetes* and in Roman ones *peregrini*, i.e. citizens without formal citizenship, whose presence, tax liability and business activities were governed by law. While the progressive expansion of the rights of strangers gave them legal protection and made it easier for them to work in the host community, it did not facilitate their acceptance. It can be said, rather, that the law on strangers, the successor to which may be seen in the law on foreigners today, created a foreign body *within* the community, and intensified tendencies of personal differentiation. Characteristic of this development is the position of Jews in Germany. A countervailing movement is represented by the development of universal human rights, the emancipation movement and the policies of naturalization and assimilation which came in the wake of the French Revolution. This line of development lives on the idea of equality, which means implicitly that the existence of inequality is denied. The attempt to meet the foreigner as an equal and to accept him as such requires him to negate his differentness and to adapt to the society and culture which receives him. Here, again, the history of the Jews is instructive. They were forcibly apprised of how flimsy was the offer of equality, and how illusory their own efforts at assimilation – just because the acknowledgement of foreigners as the other, and willingness to live with them as such, were lacking.

The continuous trend of European culture in this regard, unfortunately, is xenophobia, that is, hostility towards foreigners, a development which was occasionally enlivened, but actually merely confirmed, by periods of exoticism. Exoticism is an effusive enthusiasm for foreignness – as for things Chinese and Japanese in the eighteenth century and for the Near East in the nineteenth. This interest in, love for or, indeed, infatuation with the foreign is, in part, a sign of dissatisfaction with one's own world, and survives only as long as one can keep the foreign world concretely at arm's length: exoticism is love of the most distant. Xenophobia, by contrast, has its basis precisely in self-definition and in esteem for one's own world. It has therefore been presented as something positively natural for the constitution of self-image and community spirit: in order to value one's own world one needs to differentiate oneself from the foreign, which is therefore seen as inferior, wrong. According to this model the Greeks distinguished themselves from the barbarians, the Christians from the pagans, the civilized from savages, the white from the black, the Aryans from the Jews. In Germany, where the idea of the nation state was founded on the concept of the *Volk*, the race, the self-image of the nation state became associated with racial anthropology. Underlying this whole mindset is the notion that *homogeneity* is a prerequisite for social cohesion. Accordingly, politicians talk today of a threat to the German community on the grounds that it is being flooded and subverted by foreigners and alien races (*überfremdet und durchrasst*).

This ideology of a necessary social homogeneity has often been linked, and still is linked today, to the fear instilled by modernization. Rationalization, driven aggressively forward, produces structural unemployment and therefore a tendency to suspend the free competition for jobs. The scarce jobs are seen as *our* jobs: German jobs for the Germans. In addition, the continuing dismantling of the welfare state fuels resentment towards foreigners benefiting from it. The level of pensions is compared to the welfare benefits paid to asylum-seekers, and more and more restrictions are placed on the social equality of foreign citizens. The lack of willingness to accept the foreigners *among us*, to take an interest in them, and, in general, the inability to deal with foreignness in any way, are the foundations of a new racism. In everyday life, someone is foreign primarily if he looks foreign, and the defence mechanisms and prejudices are therefore attached to externalities. From skin colour, the colour of hair and the way it hangs, through physical form to dress customs and eating habits – such outward signs become symbols of a threat. For this reason the hostility towards foreigners, in its practical, daily application, is directed not so much at those who are aliens in terms of their legal status, but at all those who *appear foreign* through their appearance, behaviour or language, even if they are Germans. The only exception to this are certain groups of recognizable foreigners whose *equality of rank* is acknowledged, that is, in whom their assumed equality is coupled with at least a tolerance of their differentness. Characteristic of this tendency is behaviour towards Americans and Japanese. No matter how preposterously American tourists may dress and behave – as such they are acknowledged. Likewise, the different table manners and eating habits, the permanent smile and the answer hovering between yes and no are excused in a Japanese businessman. Such examples of acknowledgement of the foreign, which demonstrate in principle the possibility of different forms of behaviour, underline the fact that in general foreigners as such are not acknowledged and meet with racially tinged repulsion. Japanese and Americans are the 'good' foreigners, just as, on the basis of a general anti-Semitism, there was always talk of 'good' Jews.

This everyday racism contradicts the conception of ourselves anchored in the Basic Law. That is already enough to make it a burning moral issue. Beyond that, however, the hostility towards foreigners does not accord with our belief that we live in a modern society. The everyday behaviour towards foreigners, as well as the legislation relating to them, which treats their presence as a matter for policing, that is, as a *threat to be averted*, runs counter to the actual modernity of our society.

The unity of a modern society no longer depends on inner homogeneity, whether ethnic, linguistic or cultural. Rather, it is determined functionally, that is, it is generated by the division of labour, the market and, more recently, by technical networking. Modern society is a society of people defined in terms of work and commuting. Its cohesion is ensured by the actual involvement of its members in the system, not by a common faith, still less by a likeness of biological features, or even by a common language. It is true that the functioning of society benefits strongly from a common language. But it can be seen from many societies that this common language can have *only* this functional character – that is, it does not absolutely need to be the mother tongue of the majority – and that in principle the matter can be resolved multilingually. Religion is in any case a private affair in modern society. But even what is ordinarily called culture – art, manners, public holidays, taste – has lost its constitutive importance for modern societies. In technical civilization the central social functions are no longer organized and shaped culturally. Thus, culture, too, is turning into something private, something which belongs to the sphere of leisure, festivals and vacations. For this reason our behaviour towards foreigners and our understanding of foreignness decide, at the same time, whether we are developing a modern under-standing of society. But even if this self-understanding is still lacking, the actual modernity of society should be seen as an opportunity for putting into effect the social process of learning how to deal with foreigners.

I should like to call the customary behaviour now prevailing in dealing with foreigners the *customary behaviour of the frontier*. Just as the law relating to foreigners is essentially a law governing the entering and leaving of the country by aliens, and their permission to reside here, customary behaviour at present is of a kind which places no expectations on ourselves, but only on the others, the aliens. They are expected to adapt, to respect our laws and cus-toms, to learn our language and, especially, to present themselves in an unobtrusive way. The one-sidedness of this form of custom-ary behaviour needs to be overcome. The aim must be to develop modes of interaction which, though based on a fundamental equality as formulated in human rights, for example, at the same time imply recognition of otherness. The first step would be to establish what I would call *customary behaviour of second degree*. While this would certainly place demands on us in our way of treating foreigners, it would not yet require any interest or com-mitment or even communication concerning ourselves. It involves the traditional kind of attitude towards foreigners which, since the Enlightenment in Europe, everyone is actually supposed to have learned: respect, tolerance and courtesy. Courtesy is understood here not as any highly specific form of conduct, but as the way in which everyday communication is organized, in terms of good conduct, helpfulness, *civility* in manifesting respect and tolerance. That these requirements have not yet been turned into customary attitudes governing average everyday behaviour towards foreign-ers is in truth a scandal. It might be explained, on the one hand, by the foreigners' inability to impose sanctions – members of one's own group always have the possibility of negative sanctions if customary behaviour towards them is not respected; but it may also be explained by the fact that these requirements are mediated by reflection or even, more precisely, by abstraction: the other is respected because he or she is *also* a human being and his or her religion and culture are *also* a religion and culture like our own. This abstractness of second-degree customary behaviour could probably be remedied by engaging somewhat more with the other, the alien, by developing an interest in him or her and revealing something about one's own life. This touches on what is nowadays called multicultural learning and praxis. The reality of a pluralist and potentially multilingual society can only be done adequate justice if it becomes a matter of course that everyone learns something about other cultures during their primary socialization, grows up with at least one foreign language and participates in the practices of other cultures, through personal connections or as a guest at festivities. In this way the members of the dominant ethnic group and culture, in our case the Germans of the Christian West, will be able to recognize the narrowness of our own culture and in some cases the superior practices of others. I am thinking of such things as festival arrangements, greeting rituals and gift customs, clothing, eating habits and table manners. Education must not only impart knowledge of other cultures and religions – though it must certainly do that as well – but must make possible concrete experiences, and rehearse practical behaviour. Anti-racism cannot be limited to linguistic rules and formal equality, but must be practised from school or even kindergarten age, especially through working in multi-ethnic teams, so that it is taken for granted as a part of everyday life.

There are, however, some preconditions for this multicultural praxis and learning. They can be characterized generally as attentiveness, interest, helpfulness and, above all, the suspension of one's own claim to totality. For the difference between the foreigners and our own people consists primarily in the fact that our people form the majority and are on their own ground. True recognition of the other as other will really only be achieved when we are able to revoke this dominance and see ourselves in the role of the stranger: for *we ourselves* do not know the others' language, or their rites and customs, yet as a rule we insist that *they* learn ours. To begin with, this anomaly can only be mitigated by a helpfulness which acknowledges the difficulties of the other, the alien, and makes them our own. But it is also possible to practise taking an interest in the foreigner, being attentive to his peculiarity and problematizing our own. There is no doubt a long way to go before these attitudes will be taken for granted as what is *customary* in average behaviour. But the moral challenge currently presented by the foreigners among us can only be met in that way: not just by tolerance and equality, but by acknowledgement and interest.

— 5 —

Summary

Now that we have reached the end of this account of ethics in its historical and social context, and in the context of our present stage of civilization, it will be worthwhile to look back over what has been said. I started from a critique of philosophical ethics which, through its ambition as a special discipline, is in danger of becoming an arcane meta-ethics, or a professional game for specialists in ethical discourse. I then defined what moral questions actually are, and noted that we live in an age when moral questions are actually being posed, both for the individual and for society. Moral questions are to be seen as those through which matters become serious. A question is serious when it decides what kind of person I am, or what kind of society we live in – or how we understand our society. This gives rise to two main fields of ethics, the field of the personal life-project and the field of moral discourse. Questions which, in being answered, shape our personal life-project can only be resolved existentially. Moral questions concerning the constitution of our society are resolved by establishing social conventions which then regulate social behaviour. The field of the project of a moral life, on the one hand, and the field of moral discourse, on the other, represent the two main parts of a philosophical ethics. Between them lies the area of customary behaviour, which mediates between the two. It is a part of ethics, but not of philosophical ethics, in that customary behaviour can only be investigated empirically and can only be mediated through education.

Ethics is radically concrete; that is to say, moral questions only arise in real situations and can only be dealt with in relation to them. For this reason a large part of this book has been concerned with the general conditions of moral situations here and now. These include the historical preconditions of our society, its cultural foundations and especially its moral culture, the stage of development of civilization and, finally, the whole area of existing social conventions, from customary behaviour through laws to fundamental and human rights.

The project of a moral life is a matter for each individual. Nevertheless, the structures which a mode of living must have in order to qualify as moral can be determined in general terms. The basic requirement is that one takes one's life seriously. If one's life is to conform to a project, one must take explicit responsibility for it. That presupposes selfhood and the ability to act. As regards its content, the project of a moral life can be defined by the fact that it is concerned with *being-human-well*. Under the given conditions, this being-human-well defines itself essentially by resistance to the dangers to which humane qualities are subjected by technical civilization.

In the field of social conventions, moral questions do not arise from every regulation affecting social behaviour. Social conventions become morally relevant when they touch on our basic conception of the society in which we live, and the concept of humanity implicit in it. Such questions arise today with regard to the regulation of social behaviour towards external nature, towards the nature that we ourselves are and towards foreigners. Which other areas of social behaviour may become morally relevant is difficult to anticipate, because society's understanding of itself is never laid out fully and explicitly before us. Moreover, this self-understanding is determined not merely by the codified constitution but by society's historical conception of itself. In this way, a problem which decides a society's relationship to its own past is always a moral problem.

Finally, the question arises once more as to the connection between the different parts of ethics. While the division between questions of the moral life-project and questions of the conventions of social behaviour is an analytical one, it also characterizes, of course, a certain state of social development. It is one of the factors which mark out the present state as *modern*. To come to terms with this division it is necessary to place ethics within the concrete historical situation. That does not mean simply accepting the division. Political commitment has been mentioned as *one* link between the two spheres. One form of political commitment is to make it the content of a moral life to take a stand on certain moral questions which concern social regulations. Another possibility, of course, would be to attempt to lead an *exemplary* life, by demonstrating through one's own life certain forms of behaviour one considers correct for society as a whole, thereby becoming politically effective through one's mode of living. Both these possibilities do, however, presuppose the division between one's own life-project and social conventions. But the practical mediation between them is carried out incessantly and day by day by customary behaviour. If we have distinguished somewhat trenchantly between customary behaviour and the moral realm itself, because moral questions with regard both to one's own life and to social life present themselves precisely at the point where customary behaviour is no longer sufficient, it is nevertheless customary behaviour which places moral decisions, once taken, on a permanent footing, that is, it turns them into habits. These habits, and the resulting solidity of modes of living, reliability of character and predictability of behaviour in social life, are necessary if a project of a moral life is to become a mode of living, and if social behaviour is to conform to the basic social consensus without constant recourse to explicit rules. So, in the end, the realm of customary behaviour must be paid its due. Even though it is not the realm of true moral behaviour, it is the humus of that behaviour, the ground from which it constantly arises and to which it returns: the ethos.

Notes

Chapter 1   Introduction

1. Gernot Böhme, *Einführung in die Philosophie. Weltweisheit, Lebensform, Wissenschaft*, (Frankfurt am Main, 1997).
2. Cf. Gernot Böhme, *Der Typ Sokrates* (Frankfurt am Main, 1998).
3. Böhme, *Einführung in die Philosophie*, ch. II.1.
4. Karl-Otto Apel, *Towards a Transformation of Philosophy*, trans. Glyn Adey and David Frisby (London, 1980).
5. Karl-Otto Apel, *Diskurs und Verantwortung. Das Problem des Übergangs zur postkonventionellen Moral* (Frankfurt am Main, 1990).
6. Jürgen Habermas, *Between Facts and Norms. Contributions to a Discourse Theory of Law and Democracy*, trans. William Rehg (Cambridge, 1996).
7. Lawrence Kohlberg and Richard B. Kramer, 'Continuities and discontinuities in child and adult moral development', *Human Development* 12 (1969), pp. 93–120.
8. Ernst Tugendhat, *Vorlesungen über Ethik* (Frankfurt am Main, 1993).
9. Plato, *Protagoras*, 352a, b.
10. Plato, *Gorgias*, 470ff. Cf. my interpretation in 'Sokrates und der Tyrann', in *Der Typ Sokrates*.
11. Hans Krämer, *Integrative Ethik* (Frankfurt am Main, 1992).
12. The most dialectically advanced attempt to reconcile happiness and morality is undoubtedly that of Martin Seel in his book *Versuch über die Form des Glücks* (Frankfurt am Main, 1995). But it succeeds only if one makes an assumption which I do not share: that morality is concerned in any way with happiness.
13. Forum für Philosophie Bad Homburg (eds), *Zerstörung des moralischen Selbstbewusstseins: Chance oder Gefährdung?* (Frankfurt am Main, 1988), p. 16.
14. Ibid., p. 105 (trans. E.J.).

15. Ibid., p. 103 (trans. E.J.).
16. Ernst Tugendhat, ibid., p. 350.
17. Ibid., p. 156 (trans. E.J.).
18. It was initiated by Alasdair MacIntyre's book *After Virtue* (Notre Dame, IN, 1981). It says much about the success of this rehabilitation that a German television presenter, Ulrich Wickert, has been able to put a 'book of virtues' (*Das Buch der Tugenden*, Hamburg, 1995) on the market.
19. Gadamer sometimes translates *arete* into German as *Bestheit*. Hans-Georg Gadamer, *Ist Ethik lehrbar? Vortrag 1995* (Heidelberg, 1995).
20. Sophocles, *Antigone*, 332ff. (2nd chorus).
21. Cf. Ruthard Stäblein, *Höflichkeit. Tugend oder schöner Schein* (Bühl-Moos, 1993).
22. Norbert Elias, *The Civilizing Process*, trans. Edmund Jephcott (Oxford, and Cambridge, MA, 1994).
23. Richard Rorty's revalorization of this form of solidarity is noteworthy: *Contingency, Irony, and Solidarity* (Cambridge, 1989).
24. Hans Krämer, *Integrative Ethik* (Frankfurt am Main, 1992), p. 280.
25. Carol Gilligan, *In A Different Voice: Psychological Theory and Women's Development* (Cambridge, MA, and London, 1982).

Chapter 2   The Context of Moral Living and Argumentation

1. Immanuel Kant, *The Conflict of the Faculties*, trans. Mary J. Gregor (Lincoln, NB, and London, 1992), section 2.
2. Max Weber, *The Protestant Ethic and the Spirit of Capitalism*, trans. Talcott Parsons (London, 1985).
3. Immanuel Kant, 'An Answer to the Question: What is Enlightenment?', in James Schmidt (ed.), *What is Enlightenment? Eighteenth-Century Answers and Twentieth-Century Questions*, trans. James Schmidt (Berkeley, CA, and London, 1996), pp. 58–64.
4. Jürgen Habermas, 'Technology and Science as "Ideology"', in J. Habermas, *Towards a Rational Society*, trans. J. Shapiro (Cambridge, 1987).
5. Robert K. Merton, *On Social Structure and Science* (Chicago and London, 1996).
6. Stephen Box and Stephen Cotgrove, 'Scientific identity, occupational selections and role strain', *British Journal of Sociology* 17 (1966), pp. 20–8.
7. Gerhard Schweppenhäuser, *Ethik nach Auschwitz. Adornos negative Moralphilosophie* (Hamburg, 1993).
8. Theodor W. Adorno, *Notes to Literature*, trans. Shierry Weber Nicholsen (New York, 1991–2).
9. Adorno, *Negative Dialectics*, trans. E. B. Ashton (London, 1990).
10. Who included only three women.

11. On the Jenninger case see Armin Laschet and Heinz Malangré (eds), *Philipp Jenninger. Rede und Reaktion* (Aachen, 1989).
12. Dörte von Westernhagen, *Die Kinder der Täter. Das Dritte Reich und die Generation danach* (Munich, 1987).
13. Norbert Elias, *The Loneliness of the Dying*, trans. Edmund Jephcott (Oxford, 1985).
14. Cf. Hermann Diels, *Ancilla to the Pre-Socratic Philosophers. A Complete Translation of the Fragments in Diels's 'Fragmente der Vorsokratiker'*, trans. Kathleen Freeman (Oxford, 1948), p. 147.
15. Translated from Ruth Klüger, *Weiter leben. Eine Jugend* (Munich, 1995), p. 34.
16. Ka-Tzetnik 135633, *Shivitti – Eine Vision* (Munich, 1992), p. 84.
17. Louis Begley, *Wartime Lies* (London, 1992).
18. Cf. Victor Klemperer, *I Shall Bear Witness. The Diaries of Victor Klemperer 1942–1945*, abridged and trans. Martin Chalmers (London, 1998).
19. Ka-Tzetnik, 135633, *Shivitti*, p. 69 (trans. E.J.).
20. Hannah Arendt, *Eichmann in Jerusalem. A Report on the Banality of Evil* (Harmondsworth, 1979).
21. Ibid., p. 276.
22. Ibid., pp. 25–6.
23. Stanley Milgram, *Obedience to Authority. An Experimental View* (London, 1997).
24. Ibid., p. 6.
25. Ibid., pp. 20–1.
26. Ibid., p. 23.
27. Compare Jean-Paul Sartre's account of physical love as an interplay of sadism and masochism, in *Being and Nothingness*, trans. Hazel E. Barnes (London, 1957).
28. Sigmund Freud, *Thoughts for the Times on War and Death*, in *The Standard Edition of the Complete Psychological Works of Sigmund Freud*, trans. under the general editorship of James Strachey, vol. XIV (London, 1957), pp. 275–300. Sigmund Freud, *Civilisation and Its Discontents*, in ibid, vol. XXI (1961), pp. 64–145.
29. Quoted from Walther Hofer (ed.), *Der Nationalsozialismus. Dokumente 1933–1945*, (Frankfurt am Main, 1957), p. 114.
30. Cf. Hannah Arendt, *Eichmann in Jerusalem*.
31. Max Scheler, *Der Formalismus in der Ethik und die materiale Wertethik. Neuer Versuch der Grundlegung eines ethischen Personalismus* (Munich, 1966); Nicolai Hartmann, *Ethik* (Berlin, 1926).
32. Konrad Lorenz, *On Aggression*, trans. Marjorie Latzke (London, 1996).
33. Ibid., ch. 13, 'Ecce homo'.
34. Claude Lévi-Strauss, *Totemism*, trans. Rodney Needham (Harmondsworth, 1973); 'Totem and caste', in *The Savage Mind* (London, 1974).
35. Sigmund Freud, *Totem and Taboo* (London, 1983).
36. On Bataille's theory of prohibition and transgression, see Rita Bischof,

Souveränität und Subversion. Georges Batailles Theorie der Moderne (Munich, 1984).

37. Hans Krämer, *Integrative Ethik* (Frankfurt am Main, 1992), p. 280.
38. Hauke Brunkhorst, 'Wider den Tugendboom. Recht und Moral stützen sich nur, wenn man sie trennt', in *Frankfurter Rundschau*, 25 November 1995. Brunkhorst's use of the phrase 'solidarity towards friends' is probably directed critically against Richard Rorty, *Contingency, Irony, and Solidarity*.
39. The term was coined by Jürgen Habermas. For a more detailed analysis of the project of modernity in terms of four dimensions (nature, science, humanity, society), see Gernot Böhme, *Einführung in die Philosophie. Weltweisheit, Lebensform, Wissenschaft* (Frankfurt am Main, 1994; 2nd edn 1997).
40. The tenth commandment. The seventh and eighth commandments also relate to property.
41. Jürgen Habermas, *The Philosophical Discourse of Modernity. Twelve Lectures*, trans. Frederick Lawrence (Cambridge, 1987).
42. *Universal Declaration of Human Rights* of 11 December 1948.
43. *Konvention zum Schutze der Menschenrechte und Grundfreiheiten. Vom 4. November 1950*; translated from *Grundgesetz* (Munich, 1994).
44. Ibid.
45. *Basic Law*, Art. 1, clause 2.
46. Especially if the additional protocols are added. These are also printed in *Grundgesetz*.
47. Extract in Wolfgang Heidelmeyer, *Die Menschenrechte* (Paderborn, 1972) (trans. E.J.).
48. Karl-Otto Apel, *Towards a Transformation of Philosophy*, trans. Glyn Adey and David Frisby (London, 1980).
49. Jürgen Habermas, *Between Facts and Norms. Contributions to a Discourse Theory of Law and Democracy*, trans. William Rehg (Cambridge, 1996).
50. On this problem, see e.g. Karl F. Bertram, *Das Widerstandsrecht des Grundgesetzes*, (Berlin, 1970).
51. Ernst Tugendhat seeks to legitimize the state on the basis of social human rights, seeing it as necessary to their observance. Tugendhat, *Vorlesungen über Ethik* (Frankfurt am Main, 1993), p. 350.
52. It was somewhat different in the 'New World', where the state was not automatically presupposed as existing (Otto Vossler, 'Studien zur Erklärung der Menschenrechte', *Historische Zeitschrift* 142 (1930), pp. 515–45, esp. p. 529). See also the *Bill of Rights of Virginia* of 12 June 1776.
53. *6. Zusatzprotokoll zur Konvention der Menschenrechte und Grundfreiheiten*, Art. 2. See *Grundgesetz*, p. 99.
54. Martha Nussbaum and Amartya Sen (eds), *The Quality of Life* (Oxford, 1993).

Chapter 3   The Moral Life

1. In connection with what follows, cf. my article, 'Humanity and resistance', *Thesis Eleven* 28 (1991), pp. 70–85.
2. Ernst Tugendhat, *Vorlesungen über Ethik* (Frankfurt am Main, 1993), p. 336.
3. Ruth Klüger, *Weiter leben. Eine Jugend* (Munich, 1995), pp. 133ff.
4. Mark Twain, *Adventures of Huckleberry Finn* (New York and London, 1999).
5. Rita Bischof, *Souveränität und Subversion. Georges Batailles Theorie der Moderne* (Munich, 1984).
6. Martin Heidegger, *Being and Time*, trans. John Macquarrie and Edward Robinson (Oxford, 1967), p. 330.
7. Ibid.
8. German: *gelingendes Leben* – a standard term for the goal of ethics.
9. Cf. the well-known book by Paul Watzlawick, *The Situation Is Hopeless, But Not Serious: The Pursuit of Unhappiness* (New York and London, 1983).
10. On the interpretation of the *Hippias Minor*, see my book *Der Typ Sokrates* (Frankfurt am Main, 1988).
11. Plato, *Protagoras and Meno*, trans. W. K. C. Guthrie (Harmondsworth, 1977), p. 88.
12. Albert Camus, *The Rebel*, trans. Anthony Bower (Harmondsworth, 1990).
13. Gottfried Benn, *Der Ptolomäer*, in *Gesammelte Werke*, vol. 2, ed. Dieter Wellershoff (Wiesbaden, 1959), p. 232 (trans. E.J.).
14. Gernot Böhme, 'Leibsein als Aufgabe', in Klaus Michael Meyer-Abich and Wolfgang Krohn (eds), *Festschrift für Carl Friedrich Freiherr von Weizsäcker zum 80. Geburtstag* (Munich, 1996).
15. Emmanuel Lévinas, *Ethics and Alterity*, trans. Richard A. Cohen (Pittsburgh, 1985), p. 69.
16. Karl Marx, *Economic and Philosophic Manuscripts of 1844* (Moscow, 1967), pp. 40ff.
17. Cypora Gutnic, 'Frauen in Auschwitz. Gespräch mit Pierre Michel Klein', in Ruthard Stäblein (ed.), *Mut. Wiederentdeckung einer persönlichen Kategorie* (Darmstadt, 1993), p. 266.
18. Gernot Böhme, 'Lebensgestalt und Zeitgeschichte', *BIOS. Zeitschrift für Biographieforschung und Oral History* (1990), pp. 135–51.
19. Immanuel Kant: 'For the empirical consciousness . . . is by itself dispersed and without relation to the identity of the subject.' *Critique of Pure Reason*, trans. Paul Guyer and Allen W. Wood (Cambridge, 1997), p. 247 (B133).
20. Johan Huizinga, *Homo Ludens: A Study of the Play Element in Culture*, trans. R. F. C Hull (London, 1971).
21. Ibid., p. 26.

22. Ibid.
23. Ibid., p. 28.
24. Friedrich Schiller, *On the Aesthetic Education of Man. In a Series of Letters*, trans. Reginald Schnell (Bristol, 1994).
25. Schiller, *On the Aesthetic Education of Man*, p. 600.
26. Søren Kierkegaard, *Either/Or*, trans. H. V. and E. H. Hong (Princeton, 1987).
27. Søren Kierkegaard, *The Concept of Dread*, trans. Walter Lowrie (Princeton, 1957), pp. 123 ff.
28. For a closer analysis see Chapter III, 3, 'Existenzphilosophie' in my introduction to philosophy *Einführung in die Philosophie. Weltweisheit, Lebensform, Wissenschaft* (Frankfurt am Main, 1997).
29. The point at issue is being-human-well. Both expressions have their drawbacks: 'how well one is human' seems to presuppose a human essence; 'what kind of a person one is' seems to refer to qualities or predicates. In reality, *what* one is develops out of *how* one is.
30. Hans Jonas, *The Imperative of Responsibility: In Search of an Ethics for the Technological Age*, trans. H. Jonas and D. Herr (Chicago and London, 1984).
31. *The Holy Bible* (Authorized King James Version).

Chapter 4   Moral Argumentation

1. Garrett Hardin and John Baden (eds), *Managing the Commons* (San Francisco, 1977).
2. Immanuel Kant, *Critique of the Power of Judgement*, trans. Paul Guyer and Eric Matthews (Cambridge, 2000), §42.
3. Albert Schweitzer, *The Teaching of Reverence for Life* (London, 1966).
4. On the beginnings of animal protection legislation see Peter Singer, *Animal Liberation. A New Ethics for Our Treatment of Animals* (New York, 1975), pp. 212ff.
5. Klaus M. Meyer-Abich, 'Frieden mit den Tieren. Ein neues Verhältnis zu unseren naturgeschichtlichen Verwandten', in Klaus Franke (ed.), *Mehr Recht für Tiere* (Reinbek, 1985), pp. 7–22.
6. Heinrich Bollinger, G. Brockhaus, Joachim Hohl and H. Schwaiger, *Medizinerwelten. Die Deformation des Arztes als berufliche Qualification* (Munich, 1981).
7. *Tierschutzgesetz* of 18 August 1986 (BGBl I, p. 1319), modified by Article I of the law of 20 June 1990 (BGBl I, p. 1762).
8. Eisenhardt von Loeper, 'Bewahrung der Schöpfung und Achtung der Mitgeschöpflichkeit als Staatsziel – ein Plädoyer', in Manuel Schneider and Andreas Karrer (eds), *Die Natur ins Recht setzen. Ansätze für eine Gemeinschaft allen Lebens* (Karlsruhe, 1992), p. 247 n.
9. Ulrike Dahlke, 'Der theologische Hintergrund des Begriffs "Mitgeschöpf" in §1 TierSchG', in *Thema: 'Tierschutzethik': Tagung der*

Fachgruppe 'Tierschutzrecht und gerichtliche Veterinärmedizin (Stuttgart-Hohenheim, 1993).

10. Paul W. Taylor, *Respect for Nature. A Theory of Environmental Ethics* (Princeton, 1986).

11. Cf. Meyer-Abich, 'Frieden mit den Tieren', n. 5.

12. See my critique of Ursula Wolf's book *Das Tier in der Moral* (Frankfurt am Main, 1990), in *Merkur* 505 (1991), pp. 344–7.

13. Hans Jonas, *The Imperative of Responsibility: In Search of an Ethics for the Technological Age*, trans. H. Jonas and D. Herr (Chicago and London, 1984).

14. Regarding these historical conditions of the conception of humanity, see my book *Anthropologie in pragmatischer Hinsicht* (Frankfurt am Main, 1994).

15. Dieter Birnbacher, 'Sind wir für die Natur verantwortlich?', in D. Birnbacher (ed.), *Ökologie und Ethik* (Stuttgart, 1991), pp. 103–30; Joel Feinberg, *Die Rechte der Tiere und zukünftiger Generationen*, in idem., pp. 140–79.

16. Klaus M. Meyer-Abich, *Wege zum Frieden mit der Natur. Praktische Naturphilosophie für die Umweltpolitik* (Munich, 1984); Michel Serres, *The Natural Contract*, trans. E. MacArthur and W. Paulson (Ann Arbor, 1995).

17. Cf. the essay cited in n. 5 above.

18. Günter Altner, *Naturvergessenheit. Grundlagen einer umfassenden Bioethik* (Darmstadt, 1991).

19. In any case, Basic Law, Article 20a prudently refers only to *legal* measures, not to concrete ones.

20. Gernot Böhme, 'Die Reproduktion von Natur als gesellschaftliche Aufgabe', in Gernot Böhme and Engelbert Schramm (eds), *Soziale Naturwissenschaft. Wege zu einer Erweiterung der Ökologie* (Frankfurt am Main, 1985), pp. 93–107.

21. It would not be enough to say in Article 20a: 'the state *protects and develops the natural foundations of life*' since the latter need in some cases to be completely restored. Cf. my article 'Die Natur herstellen. Der Zustand unserer natürlichen Lebensbedingungen als unser geschichtlicher Ort', *Frankfurter Rundschau*, 5 August 1995.

22. In the essay 'Die Konsitution der Natur durch Arbeit', in Böhme and Schramm (eds), *Soziale Naturwissenschaft*, pp. 43–62.

23. Hans Immler, 'Die Natur ins wirtschaftliche Recht setzen. Argumente für eine ökologische Ökonomie', in Schneider and Karrer (eds), *Die Natur ins Recht setzen*, pp. 73–85.

24. Reprinted in Arthur J. Brock, *Greek Medicine* (London and Toronto, 1972), p. 35.

25. In fact, however, it was contained in the Hippocratic oath: 'nor . . . will I give a destructive pessary to a woman' (ibid.).

26. *Strafgesetzbuch* (Munich, 1994) (Beck-Texte im dtv), Introduction, p. XXVII.

27. Michael Piazolo, *Das Recht auf Abtreibung als Teilaspekt des Right of Privacy* (Frankfurt am Main, 1982).
28. Translated from 'Reform des §218. Aus der öffentlichen Anhörung des Sonderausschusses für die Strafrechtsreform des Deutschen Bundestages', *Zur Sache* 6/72 (Deutscher Bundestag: Presse- und Informationszentrum, 1972), p. 174.
29. Translated from Norbert Hoerster, *Abtreibung im säkularen Staat. Argumente gegen den § 218* (Frankfurt am Main, 1991), p. 116.
30. Translated from Anselm Hertz, 'Moraltheologische und strafrechtliche Argumente zum Schutz des werdenden Lebens', in Jürgen Baumann (ed.), *Das Verbot des §218* (Darmstadt, 1972), p. 92.
31. Ibid., p. 90, referring to *Summa Theologiae*, I–II, q. 96 a2, a3.
32. Some are reproduced in Hans-Martin Sass (ed.), *Medizin und Ethik* (Stuttgart, 1989).
33. Hermann Schmid, 'Gentherapie aus juristischer Sicht – schweizerische und internationale Tendenzen', in Christoph Rehmann-Sutter and Hansjakob Müller (eds), *Ethik und Gentherapie. Zum praktischen Diskurs um die molekulare Medizin* (Tübingen, 1995), pp. 137–53.
34. 'Entwurf der Bioethik-Deklaration', printed in *Frankfurter Rundschau*, 14 August 1995, Dokumentation. English text in *Eubios. Journal of Asian and International Bioethics* 6 (1995), pp. 58–9. Revised draft: *Avant-Projet de déclaration universelle sur le génome humain et les droits de la personne humaine* (Paris, UNESCO, 4 March 1996).
35. The 1995 draft even spoke of a 'reduction of inequality throughout the world'.
36. See my book *Einführung in die Philosophie. Weltweisheit, Lebensform, Wissenschaft* (Frankfurt am Main, 1998), ch. I.2 – I.6.
37. From Schmid, 'Gentherapie aus juristischer Sicht', p. 139 (trans. E.J.).
38. Ibid., p. 151 (trans. E.J.).
39. Christoph Rehmann-Sutter, 'Politik der genetischen Identität. Gute und schlechte Gründe, auf Keimbahntheorie zu verzichten', in Christoph Rehmann-Sutter and Hansjakob Müller (eds), *Ethik und Gentherapie*, p. 187 (trans. E.J.).
40. Ibid., pp. 180ff.
41. Peter Weingart, Jürgen Kroll and Kurt Bayertz, *Rasse, Blut und Gene. Geschichte der Eugenik und Rassenhygiene in Deutschland* (Frankfurt am Main, 1988).
42. Translated from Tom L. Beauchamp, 'Antwort auf Rachels zum Thema Euthanasie', in Hans-Martin Sass (ed.), *Medizin und Ethik*, p. 274.
43. Wolfgang van den Daele, *Mensch nach Maß? Ethische Probleme der Genmanipulation und Gentherapie* (Munich, 1985).
44. Regarding this difference between traditional and modern societies, see Talcott Parsons and Edward A. Shils (eds), *Towards a General Theory of Action* (Cambridge, MA, 1967), pp. 80ff.
45. *Deutsches Ausländerrecht* (Beck-Texte), 13th edn (Introduction by Prof.

Helmut Rittstieg), (Munich, 2000). See, in particular, §4 of the Law of Citizenship (*Staatsangehörigkeitsgesetz*).
46. Daniel Cohn-Bendit and Thomas Schmid, *Heimat Babylon. Das Wagnis der multikulturellen Demokratie* (Hamburg, 1992), pp. 320–1.
47. Cf. Ursula Münch, *Asylpolitik in der Bundesrepublik Deutschland. Entwicklung und Alternativen* (Opladen, 1992), pp. 19ff.
48. Translated from Kurt R. Grossmann, *Emigration. Die Geschichte der Hitler-Flüchtlinge 1933–1945* (Frankfurt am Main, 1969), pp. 9ff.
49. *Der völkerrechtliche Rahmen für die Reform des deutschen Asylrechts*, compiled by Jochen A. Frowein and Andres Zimmermann (Cologne (*Bundesanzeiger*), 1993).
50. United Nations, 1951 Convention Relating to the Status of Refugees (28 July 1951).
51. This formulation was taken over as §51 in the law on aliens of 1990.

Helmut Rittstieg), (Munich, 2000). See, in particular, §4 of the Law of Citizenship (*Staatsangehörigkeitsgesetz*).

46. Daniel Cohn-Bendit and Thomas Schmid, *Heimat Babylon. Das Wagnis der multikulturellen Demokratie* (Hamburg, 1992), pp. 320–1.

47. Cf. Ursula Münch, *Asylpolitik in der Bundesrepublik Deutschland. Entwicklung und Alternativen* (Opladen, 1992), pp. 19ff.

48. Translated from Kurt R. Grossmann, *Emigration. Die Geschichte der Hitler-Flüchtlinge 1933–1945* (Frankfurt am Main, 1969), pp. 9ff.

49. *Der völkerrechtliche Rahmen für die Reform des deutschen Asylrechts*, compiled by Jochen A. Frowein and Andres Zimmermann (Cologne (*Bundesanzeiger*), 1993).

50. United Nations, 1951 Convention Relating to the Status of Refugees (28 July 1951).

51. This formulation was taken over as §51 in the law on aliens of 1990.